Psychological Foundations of Education

Psychological Foundations of Education

JAGDISH CHAND
Former Deputy Director of Education and
Executive Director of the Delhi Bureau of Textbooks,
Delhi Administration

ANSHAH
Anshah Publishing House

Rs. 795

ISBN: 978-81-8364-062-6

2014 Impression
2010

Psychological Foundation of Education

Published by:

ANSHAH PUBLISHING HOUSE
LG 18-19, Pankaj Central Market,
Patparganj, Delhi 110092, Ph.: 22235152, 22236152km
Email: info@shiprapublication.com
Website: www.shiprapublication.com

Preface

The book 'Psychological Philosophical and Sociological Foundations of Education', published in 2009 covers the emerging concerns in education presented by the changing Philosophical, Psychological and Sociological perspectives.

As per the demand in the market and requirement of curriculum in various universities, the book covering Psychological Foundations of Education is brought out independently. It is hoped that this volume will be welcomed by the readers and its advantage is also taken by the pre-service and in-service teachers.

Wide range of primary and secondary sources has been consulted and used for enriching the book, author is grateful to all the authors and their publishers.

Jagdish Chand

Contents

1

Meaning, Definition and Significance of Educational Psychology

MEANING AND DEFINITION OF EDUCATIONAL PSYCHOLOGY

Educational psychology is the applied branch of psychology in an educational setting. In simple words, it implies the application of principles and practices of psychology to the various dimensions of education with a view to modify the behaviour in an educational environment so that he may amicably adjust himself with the society with maximum confidence, satisfaction and security.

Important definitions are given below so as to understand the true meaning of educational psychology in its various facets:

1. *The Encyclopaedia of Educational Research* states, "Educational psychology is the study of the learner and of the learning-teaching process in its various (branches) directed towards helping the child come to terms with society with a maximum of security and satisfaction".
2. *Stephen* regards educational psychology as "the systematic study of the educational growth and development of a child".
3. *Judd* considers educational psychology as "the science which explains the changes that take place in the individuals as they pass through the various stages of development".
4. According to *Skinner*, "Educational psychology is that branch of psychology which deals with teaching and learning". He further observes, "Educational psychology covers the entire range and behaviour of the personality as related to education".

5. *Crow* and *Crow* put it as, "Educational psychology describes and explains the learning experiences of an individual from birth through old age".
6. *E.A. Peel* considers educational psychology as the "Science of Education".
7. In the words of *Anderson*, "While general psychology is a pure science, educational psychology is its application in the field of education with the aim of socialising an individual and modifying his behaviour".
8. In the words of *Trow*, "Educational psychology is the study of psychological aspects of educational situation".
9. According to *Walter B. Kolesnik*, "Educational psychology is the study of those facts and principles of psychology which help to explain and improve the process of education".

Summing up: A perusal of the above definitions would indicate that the definitions given by Anderson Kolesnik and '*The Encyclopaedia of Educational Research*' provide the true meaning of educational psychology. Other definitions, by and large, put emphasis on 'Study' but do not emphatically state the ultimate aim of studying. A mere study of the behaviour of the learner is not enough unless it is related to the modification of the behaviour towards desired ends.

From these it is concluded that educational psychology is that applied branch of psychology which studies the experiences and behaviours of the learners in relation to educational environment which is mainly provided by the teacher. Therefore, educational psychology becomes a psychology of teaching and learning. Teaching and learning are the main processes of education and the learner is a key figure in the process.

NATURE OF EDUCATIONAL PSYCHOLOGY

Following points bring out the nature of educational psychology. Some of the points overlap:

1. Educational psychology is an applied science.
2. Educational psychology is a social science.
3. Educational psychology is a positive science.
4. Educational psychology is a specific science.

5. Educational psychology is a developing and growing science.
6. Educational psychology is an academic discipline.
7. Educational psychology is not as exact as natural and physical sciences.

SCOPE OF EDUCATIONAL PSYCHOLOGY

Scope of educational psychology is as vast as the scope of education itself. Gates and others have very aptly remarked, "The boundaries of educational psychology are uncertain and changing". The exposition of 'Information Technology' (IT) has been exercising a far-reaching influence on the scope of educational psychology. New and novel situations need new and novel approaches to educational matters. Nevertheless, we may mention the most significant areas of the scope of educational psychology.

Classification I: Broad Areas

1. *Learner: Growth and Development.*
   (a) Heredity and environment affecting the learner.
   (b) General growth and development of the learner at different stages of education.
   (c) Emotional, intellectual and social development of the learner.
   (d) Individual differences of the learners.
   (e) Learner's aptitudes, interests and intelligence
2. *Learning*
   (a) Concept of learning.
   (b) Process of learning.
   (c) Primary and concomitant learning.
   (d) Domains of learning: Cognitive, Affective and Psychomotor.
   (e) Factors affecting learning.
   (f) Transfer of training.
   (g) Learning situations.
   (h) Forgetting.
   (i) Remembering.
   (j) Learning span.

(k) Theories of learning.
(l) Practices of learning.

3. *Personality and Adjustment*
(a) Emotions.
(b) Mental health of the learner.
(c) Mental health of the teacher.
(d) Character development.
(e) Social interaction.

4. *Evaluation and Measurement*
(i) Meaning of the concepts of evaluation and measurement.
(ii) Basic principles of evaluation and measurement.
(iii) Measurement of aptitudes, attitudes and intelligence.
(iv) Measurement of learning.
(v) Measures of adjustment.
(vi) Applications of the results of measurement and evaluation.

5. *Techniques and Methods in Educational Psychology*
(a) Scientific study of educational problems.
(b) Statistical techniques.
(c) Implications of research for the classroom teacher.

Classification II

(1)	(2)	(3)	(4)	(5)	(6)
The Learner (Pupil)	The Learning Experiences	The Learning Environment or Situation	The Learning Process	The Teaching Situation	Evaluation of Learning Experience

1. *The Learner*: This includes the study of growth and development of the individual in various aspects of his personality – physical, mental, social and emotional.

   This includes the study of the abilities, needs of motivational forces and anxiety of the individual learner as well as the difference that exist among different individuals.

2. *Learning Experiences*: This includes providing activities and subjects according to the maturity level of the students.

3. *The Learning Situation*: In the learning situation, educational

psychology studies such factors as classroom management and discipline, techniques and aids which facilitate learning, methods of teaching, evaluation techniques and practices, guidance and counselling.

4. *The Learning Process*: In the learning process, educational psychology deals with the nature of learning and how it takes place. It considers the various theoretical view points as well as experimental evidences to explain the role and nature of reinforcement, forgetting, problem solving, transfer of training and the learning of concepts, skills and attitudes.
5. *The Teaching Situation*: Effectiveness of educational psychology becomes relevant only when its methods and findings become a part of educational practices when the teachers apply psychological methods.
6. *Evaluation of Learning Experiences*: In recent years, evaluation of learning experiences has assumed great significant in the subject-matter of psychology.

'When to Teach', 'What to Teach', and 'How to Teach'—Questions of Educational Psychology

Educational psychologists are more concerned with the answer of these questions. The first question refers to the developmental processes that gradually mature as the child grows up. Similarly the problem of what to teach is important because of its close relationship with the process of maturation. Certain types of learning can be useful to the child only when he has matured sufficiently in certain faculties. We cannot think of teaching mathematics to a three year child, though he may be taught to count simple things. The problem of how to teach is equally important because there are ways and means of teaching which can make the education of a child more effective, meaningful and useful.

SIGNIFICANCE OF EDUCATIONAL PSYCHOLOGY TO TEACHERS

The work of the teacher is like that of a gardener to a great extent. The gardener needs the knowledge of the plant life. The teacher also needs the knowledge of the learner. It is the duty of the gardener to ensure that all the plants grow and yield good flowers and fruits and he can do so when he is well-acquainted with all the details about them. The objective of the teacher is to ensure that all the learners under his care and charge develop into happy and healthy personalities and he can do so only when he knows how the learners develop and behave. This knowledge is provided to the teacher by educational psychology.

The work of the teacher may also be compared to that of an artist who must know his material thoroughly if he wants to produce a fine piece of art. What will happen to the artist if he starts his work without fully understanding the kind of material he has to work with. The teacher as an artist, is not only required to know the subject-matter but also to know the child's nature and the techniques of moulding his behaviour in accordance with the objectives.

The work of the teacher assume all the more significance and needs more delicacy and expertness than that of the gardener and the artist as here, human beings are involved.

R.A. Davis in '*Applicability and Applications of Psychology with Particular Reference to Classroom Learning*' (1943) has pointed out the significance of educational psychology as, "Psychology has made a distinct contribution to education through its analysis of pupil potentialities and differences as revealed by means of various types of psychological tests. It has also contributed directly to the knowledge of pupil growth and maturation during the school years".

G.M. Blair in '*The Psychological Interpretation of Teaching*' (1947) has stated the importance of educational psychology to the teacher in these words, "Modern teacher, if he is to succeed with his work should be a specialist who understands children, how they grow, develop, learn and adjust. He should be diagnostician, who can discover special difficulties of children and at the same time possesses the requisite skill for carrying forward the necessary remedial work. He should also be performing important educational and vocational guidance functions. No person untrained in the methods of psychology can possibly fulfil the obligations and tasks which are the responsibilities of the teacher".

Principles and practices of educational psychology are needed by the teacher on account of the following considerations:

1. *Knowledge of John and Latin (Knowledge of the Learner and the Subject-matter) Equally Necessary*: Sir John Adams has put it thus in his book '*New Teaching*'. The verbs of teaching govern two accusatives, one of the person and another of the thing as, 'the master taught John Latin'." He says that there are two definite subjects—John, the student and Latin the subject which are governed by the verb taught". Now the teacher must understand both John as well as Latin if he wants to make 'teaching' effective. Educational psychology helps him in understanding 'John'. He may be a great scholar of Latin but he will not succeed in teaching Latin to John if he has no knowledge of the mental set up of John. Acquisition of knowledge is now no more the main object of education but it is still very significant in the process of education. Acquisition of knowledge is also a sort of modification in the behaviour of the child. For this purpose the educator will have to consider the mental process of the child and not only the quality of knowledge which he is going to put into the living mind.

2. *Knowledge of Individual Differences*: No two persons are exactly alike. There is individual difference. Pupils always differ in their level of intelligence, aptitudes, likes and dislikes and in other propensities and potentialities. Different minds are to be trained by the teacher. There are gifted, backward, retarded, talented and handicapped children. All of them should not be treated in the same manner. Knowledge of educational psychology helps the teacher to cater to individual differences of children.

3. *Educational Psychology and Process of Learning*: Teaching and learning go side by side. All education depends upon the learning of new responses and the capacity of a human child to learn new responses. Educational psychology discusses the nature of learning theories and types of learning for different age levels and situations. Therefore, knowledge of educational psychology becomes essential to a teacher to study all these problems.

4. *Knowledge of Educational Psychology Helpful in Providing a Scientific Attitude to the Teachers*: The knowledge of psychology can make the teacher more scientific in his educational practices and consequently he will be more objective and methodical in his work.

5. *Educational Psychology Useful in the Methods of Teaching*: Educational psychology has discovered many secrets about mental

forces. Recent researches made in the field of educational psychology give us valuable suggestions for better methods of teaching and memorising, for making desirable habits and eradicating anti-social tendencies. Educational psychology tells us how significant play and recreation are for the children and how play-way and project methods turn the work of learning into an interesting play.

6. *Educational Psychology Helpful in Changing the Outlook and Attitude of the Teacher Towards His Pupils*: The knowledge of psychology can change the outlook and attitude of the teacher towards children by understanding them adequately.

7. *Educational Psychology Helping the Teacher in His Own Mental Development*: The study of educational psychology can help the teacher to understand himself. He will realise his own merits and weaknesses and make attempts to overcome his weaknesses.

8. *Educational Psychology and Nervous System*: The entire education depends on the function of the brain and nervous system. It becomes essential for a teacher to study the nervous system which controls human behaviour. He must have the knowledge of sensory organs which are the gateways of knowledge.

9. *Educational Psychology and Play*: Play is a natural tendency having great educational potentials. Knowledge of educational psychology helps the teacher to provide for a variety of activities for children.

10. *Educational Psychology Measurements are very Useful for the Teacher*: Educational psychology has made many strides in this respect quite recently. It has produced many reliable tests and instruments of mental measurement. These are proving to be extremely useful in the field of education. We can quite easily measure mental capacities, basic intelligence, temperamental attitudes and special inclinations of children and base educational programmes on these findings. These measurements show that all the children differ and that every child is a unique being. The teacher can know that children with I.Q. below 90 cannot do well in medical, engineering, administrative or other similar vocations. But he knows that such young ones are not doomed if they cannot do well in intellectual callings. He can easily explore some other fields where such children can also flourish.

11. *Character Development*: Educational psychology helps a lot to

the formation and development of character. The teacher comes to know the methods he should adopt in inculcating suitable character traits, and moral principles among the children.

12. *Educational Psychology and Productive Activities*: A great stress is being laid these days on work experience and socially useful productive work. Educational psychology helps the teacher to know how various activities in these fields can be used for the fulfilment of the basic needs of children.

13. *Educational Psychology Useful in Guidance and Counselling*: Students need various types of guidance and counselling. A teacher with the knowledge of educational psychology can render very useful service.

14. *Educational Psychology Useful to the Teacher in Realisation of the Aims of Education*: The main aim of education is the harmonious and all-round development of the educand. Development comes from within and the inner potentialities must be understood and approached for the desired modification in the development of the child. The knowledge of educational psychology helps the teacher to understand the inner potentialities which underlie the behaviour of the child.

IMPORTANCE OF EDUCATIONAL PSYCHOLOGY TO DIFFERENT SECTIONS

Educational psychology, being functional in its character is very helpful to all sections of society engaged in pursuing different dimensions of education at all levels of education, i.e., formal, non-formal and informal.

Educational psychology is of great importance to parents, teachers, guidance workers, career masters, and psychoanalysts etc.

According to *W.A. Kelly* (1941), educational psychology is helpful in the following ways:

1. It provides a knowledge of the nature of the child.
2. It gives understanding of the nature, aims and purposes of education.
3. It gives understanding of the scientific methods and procedures which have been used in arriving at the facts and principles of educational psychology.

4. It presents the principles and techniques of learning and teaching.
5. It gives training in methods of measuring abilities and achievement in school subjects.
6. It provides a knowledge of the growth and development of children.
7. It assists in the better adjustment of children and helps to prevent maladjustment.
8. It helps to understand the significance and control of emotions.
9. It gives an understanding of the principles and techniques of correct training.

IMPORTANCE OF EDUCATIONAL PSYCHOLOGY TO PARENTS

An elementary knowledge of educational psychology would prove very useful to the parents who are undoubtedly the first teachers in the following manners:

1. The knowledge of educational psychology points out to the parents that they should show reasonable amount of love and affection to their children. They should bear in mind the maxim, "Love the child and the child will love you. Hate the child and he will hate you".
2. It helps the parents to understand the process of development and growth of their children.
3. Educational psychology acquaints the parents with the emotional, mental and physical needs of the children.
4. Educational psychology impresses upon the parents of the necessity of providing wholesome environment to the children so that they lead a happy life and are free of anxiety.
5. Educational psychology enables the parents to know that they should not take resource to repression and punishment which adversely affect the mental health of children.
6. Educational psychology enables the parents to observe keenly the behaviour of children. It enables them to control their habits.
7. It helps the parents to understand themselves, their roles and responsibilities towards their children.

2

Human Growth and Development: Significance, Characteristics and Principles/ Stages—Educational Implications

SIGNIFICANCE OF CHILD DEVELOPMENT

Children constitute a nation's future human resources. It is, therefore, very important that their welfare receives the highest importance.

India's commitment to the cause of children is as old as its civilisation. The child is believed to be a gift of God. He must be nurtured with care and affection within the family and the society.

The development of the child should receive all the more attention in Indian scenario as here child population constitutes nearly 34 per cent of the total population (nearly 15 per cent up to the age of 6 years and 19 per cent between 6 and 14 years of age). This is the most crucial and vulnerable period of life. The foundations of future are laid at this stage. Naturally, the foundation must be stable and strong.

The great Indian economist Amartya Sen reminds us, 'You reap what you sow and you don't reap what you do not sow". Now it is the time to sow properly the future of this great Indian nation by investing properly in children.

On account of the paramount importance of child development, the UNO adopted the Convention on the Rights of the Child (CRC) on November 20, 1989. India ratified this Convention in 1992.

The Convention recognises that the child, for the full and harmonious development of his or her personality, should grow up in a family environment, in an atmosphere of happiness, love and understanding.

Article 28 of CRC recognises the right of the child to education.

Article 29 states that the education of the child, shall be directed to the development of the child's personality, talents, mental and physical abilities to their fullest potential.

The Convention proclaims that childhood is entitled to special care and assistance.

SOME PROMINENT EDUCATORS AND THINKERS ON THE DEVELOPMENT AND EDUCATION OF CHILDREN

A. Indian Thinkers

It is the highest duty of parents, teachers and relatives to adorn children with good education, noble character, refined manners and amiable temper.

—Swami Dayanand (1825-1883), *'Satyarth Prakash'*

No one was ever really taught. Each of us has to teach himself. You can supply the growing seed with the materials for the making up of its body, bringing to it the earth, the water, the air that it wants. And there your work stops. So with the education of the child. —Swami Vivekanand (1863-1902), *'The Complete Works of Swami Vivekanand, Vol. V'*

To say good words, give wise advice to a child has very little effect, if one does not show by one's loving example the truth of what one teaches.

—Sri Aurobindo (1872-1950), *'The Supramental Manifestation', 1952*

I now clearly see the mistake is to judge boys by the standard of grown-ups, children are living beings—more living than grown up people. The child learns so easily because it has a natural gift. But adults, because they are tyrants, ignore natural gifts and say that children must learn through the process as themselves. This is one of man's most cruel, most wasteful mistakes.

—Rabindranath Tagore (1861-1941), *'Personality'*

By education, I mean an all-round drawing out of the best in child and man—body, mind and spirit. I would develop in the child his hands, his brain and his soul.

—Mahatma Gandhi (1869-1948), *'Basic Education'*

Heaven is in the happiness of the child.

—Gijubhai Badheka (1885-1939), *Education in Primary School in Hindi*

Unfortunately in our schools we look upon children as mere raw stuff on which we can impose our unjust views through our powerful wills. We must liberate the young from the blind despotism of the old. We must not destroy his right and power of self-direction.

—Dr. Sarvapalli Radhakrishnan (1888-1975), *'Occasional Speeches and Writings, 1956'.*

In the training of our teachers for various kinds of schools, they should be provided with the technique of such competent observation as will enable them to understand their pupils and direct their educational work in the light of this understanding.

—Dr. Zakir Hussain (1897-1969), *'Educational Reconstruction, 1958'*

B. Western Thinkers

Let our maxim be to follow the laws of nature in all things.

If the teacher's skill cannot make any impression, his blows will have no effect.

—John Comenius (1592-1670), known for his publication *'Great Didactic'.*

Begin by making a careful study of your scholars (Children).

—Jean Jacques 'Rousseau' (1712-1778)

I wish to psychologise education.

Teach him (child) nothing by words that you teach him by things themselves. —John Heinrich Pestalozzi (1746-1827)

Play is the highest phase of child development. It is the purest, most spiritual activity of man at this stage. It gives, therefore, joy, freedom, contentment, inner and outer rest, peace with the world.

—Fredrich Froebel (1782-1852)

The secret of education lies in respecting the child.

—Ralph Waldo Emerson (1802-1882)

The pupil is immature and helpless and he must not be given a long rope with which he may hang himself. —W.C. Bagley (1874-1946)

Education must begin with a psychological insight into the child's capacities and interests. The curriculum must grow out of child's interests, experiences, impulses and needs. —John Dewey (1857-1950)

Child is a body which grows and a soul which develops—these two forms—physical and psychic, have one eternal form, life itself. We must neither mar nor stifle the mysterious powers which lie between these two forms of growth. The school must permit the free, natural manifestations of the child. —Maria, Montessori (1870-1952)

MEANING OF HUMAN DEVELOPMENT

The primary aim of education is the development of the whole child (Fig. 2.1) which implies well-balanced personality; aesthetically sound, culturally defined, emotionally stable, mentally alert, morally upright, physically strong, socially efficient, spiritually enlightened, vocationally self-sufficient and internationally liberal. It is, therefore, very important to understand the meaning of development, its very dimensions, factors influencing development and the role of the teacher and the school in this task.

In the words of *A. Angyal*, "Development cannot be considered in terms of the mind alone but rather in terms of the individual as a whole in relationship with his experience with others". *J.E. Anderson* explains development as, "Development does not consist merely of adding inches to one's height or improving one's ability. Instead development is a complex process of integrating many structures and functions".

In the words of *E.B. Hurlock*, "Development means a progressive series of change that occur in an orderly predictable pattern as a result of maturation and experience".

DISTINCTION BETWEEN GROWTH AND DEVELOPMENT

The terms growth and developments are often used interchangeably but they are conceptually different. According to *L.D. Crow* and *A. Crow* (1962), growth refers to structural and

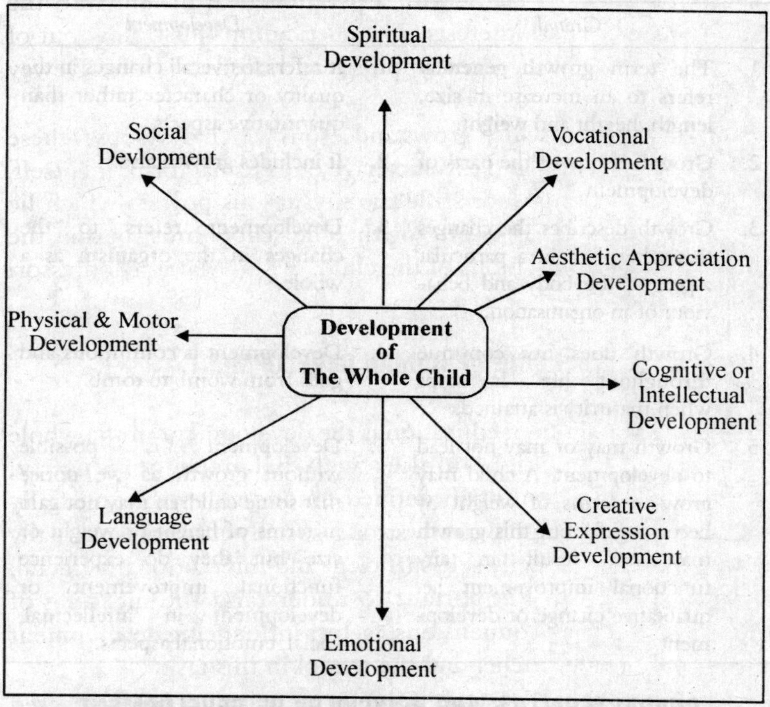

Fig. 2.1: The Figure Illustrates the Various Aspects/Patterns of the Development of the Learner

physiological changes whereas development is concerned with growth as well as those changes in behaviour which result from environment. Usually growth contributes to development but not always.

In general growth refers change in size and body—bones, muscles etc.

Maturity involves qualitative change.

Development involves a series of progressive, orderly and meaningful changes leading to the goals of maturity.

As the child grows, his mind and body mature and he is able to function at a higher level. Development is a product of maturation and learning.

	Growth		Development
1.	The term growth generally refers to an increase in size, length, height and weight.	1.	It refers to overall changes in the quality or character rather than quantitative aspects.
2.	Growth is one of the parts of development.	2.	It includes growth also.
3.	Growth describes the changes that take place in a particular aspect of the body and behaviour of an organisation.	3.	Development refers to the changes in the organism as a whole.
4.	Growth does not continue throughout life. It stops when maturity is attained.	4.	Development is continuous and goes from womb to tomb.
5.	Growth may or may not lead to development. A child may grow in terms of weight by becoming fat but this growth may not result in any functional improvement i.e. qualitative change or development.	5.	Development is possible without growth as we notice that some children may not gain in terms of height or weight or size but they do experience functional improvement or development in intellectual, social, emotional aspects.

CHARACTERISTICS AND PRINCIPLES OF DEVELOPMENT

Following are the general principles of growth and development of individuals:

1. *The Principle of Individual Differences*: There are individual differences in the development of children. The difference is mostly in the intellectual capacity of all human beings. Difference in special aptitudes is most marked among children. This is caused by differences in heredity, endowments and environment.

2. *Principle of Continuous Growth and Development Process*: The growth and development starts from the moment of conception of the individual in the mother's womb and continues till he reaches his grave. It is a continuous stream of development. Development proceeds by stages but it is a continuous process. Changes in the patterns of body and behaviour take place throughout life. Emergence of each type of behaviour is dependent on the development that has gone before.

3. *Principle of Uneven Tempo of Growth and Development*: Growth and development though is continuous, yet its rate of development is in fits and starts and not uniform at all times. In the earlier stages it is quick, but slows down in later years of infancy. Again at the state of puberty, there is a sudden rise in the growth and development.

4. *Principle of Uniformity of Development Pattern*: Although development has individual differences, yet it follows a definite sequence common to the off-springs of human beings. The outstanding example is that off-springs develop their head first and other parts of the body later on. Motor and language development in human off-springs has a definite sequence.

5. *Principle of Development from General to Specific Responses*: If we examine the different developmental aspects of the child we will find that general activity precedes specific activity in all his/her actions. The movements of the child are of general nature in the beginning but later on they become specific.

6. *Principle of Interrelation*: It has been observed that the growth and development in various aspects like physical, mental, social, etc. are inter-related and interdependent. Growth and development of the child in one aspect leads to the development in other aspects as well. It has also been observed that children who are highly intelligent, generally have a robust health, whereas children with lower intelligence have weak health and regress in their emotional and social development.

7. *Principle of Developmental Direction*: There are two important principles of development: (a) Cephalo-cadal, and (b) Proximo-distal.

By cephalo-cadal development we mean that it has a longitudinal axis, i.e., that human development is from head to foot. This implies that control of the body as well as improvement in the structure itself, develops first in the head and progresses later to parts further from head. Another example of this aspect of development is that a child can lift his head by his neck before he can do so by lifting his chest.

The proximo-distal tendency means that child develops from the centre of the body, i.e., the spinal chord to the periphery of the body, i.e., fingers. In the beginning, the child is able to control his large fundamental muscles and smaller muscles later on. The outstanding example is that the control over fingers comes after control over the arm and the hand.

8. *Principle of Integration*: This principle implies that the development of the child is both from general to specific and specific to general. The child while busy in his specific activities arrives at a general rule. Again he gives a tryout of his general rule on certain specific activities. Thus, the development of the child integrates both general and specific activities.

9. *Principle of Predictability of Development*: We know that every child develops in his own way and develops nearly constantly. It is with this presumption that we can also predict his future range of development. This prediction is only possible in the case of children of average or normal development. We shall not be able to predict in the case of abnormal or highly intelligent children.

10. *Principle of Spiral and Non-Linear Development*: This principle implies that the development of the child is not in a straight line (linear) but it is in the form of a cork-screw (spiral). He advances in his development in one period but takes rest in the following period. This enables him to consolidate his development.

11. *The Principle of Struggle*: While the child is developing up towards maturity there are conflicting impulses and demands. The child struggles against these in his striving for maturity.

12. *The Principle of Indigenous Motivation*: As the child matures in his capacities of doing, thinking and feeling, he has an impulse to put them to use and he does it wholeheartedly. This has been described by *Jersild* as 'Indigenous Motivation'.

13. *The Principle of Anticipation*: The child in his/her process of development also uses his capacity of self-repair. He modifies his behaviour and even habits keeping in view what he is going 'to become' in future. Thus, he consciously anticipates his future direction of development.

14. *The Principle of Interaction between Heredity and Environment*: The development of the child is a product of both. This is true at all times and stages of his development.

EDUCATIONAL IMPLICATIONS OF THE PRINCIPLES OF DEVELOPMENT

A knowledge of principles of growth and development will enlighten the parents and teachers on the potentialities of their children. They should, therefore, provide suitable opportunities for the maximum development of their children. For planning and implementing suitable programmes for the all-round development of children, following guidelines may be taken into consideration:

1. *Need for Paying Attention to Individual Differences of the Learners*: The parents and teachers should keep in view that there are individual variations in the rates of growth and every child develops in a unique way. Hence they should pay individual attention to every child. It stipulates the provision of diversified courses and provision of all activities according to needs and interests of various stages of growth.
2. *Need for Developing Motivation*: Teachers should organise teaching-learning programmes, procedures and practices according to the maturational levels of children.
3. *Need for a Pragmatic Outlook*: Every stage of growth has its possibilities and limitations. Teachers and parents should not place undue demands on the child. Such demands lead to mental tension for the child.
4. *Need for Correlation*: Teachers should keep in mind that children develop on the principle of interrelatedness of development growth. It is, therefore, necessary for them to search for the principle of correlation.
5. *Influence of Heredity and Environment*: Parents and teachers should keep in view that it is difficult to change the heredity of the child but environment can be modified.
6. *Emphasis on Doing*: 'Doing' helps in the development of mental, physical and social skills.
7. *Creativity Aspect*: Children are creative and they need assistance and guidance to develop their creativity.
8. *Individual Attention*: Each child needs attention and a neglected child in the home or in the class loses interest in work and play.

9. *Different Modes of Teaching-Learning*: Singing songs and learning rhymes, drawing pictures and reading stories help the child's mind to grow at the pre-primary, primary and middle stages.
10. *Recognition Aspect*: For proper development, all children need adequate praise and recognition for their work.
11. *Satisfaction of Curiosity*: Children are curious to learn and respond with interest to new things.
12. *Reasonable Repetition*: Children learn through repetition; of course excessive repetition tends to kill interest.
13. *Need-Satisfaction at Each Stage*: Each stage in the development of an individual has developmental needs peculiar to it and these must be taken note of.
14. *Observation*: Observation of children leads to better understanding on the part of parents and teachers.
15. *Clarity*: When parents and teachers speak clearly, use appropriate words and adopt a proper style and manner, children are likely to do the same.
16. *Healthy Environment*: Children need an environment which promotes initiative and trust.
17. *Consistency and Firmness*: Consistency, firmness, love and patience on the part of parents and teachers will go a long way in the wholesome development of children.
18. *Human Relations*: Children need close, loving and sensitive relationships with the adults who are charged with the responsibility of looking after them. The feeling of being wanted and loved in the children is vital to their inner development. Children need a sense of security which should be provided by parents and teachers. Anger and violence are damaging to the inner development of the children. Healthy relationships established in the earlier stages of life help to set the pattern of future development.

INTERRELATIONSHIPS AND INTERDEPENDENCE OF VARIOUS PATTERNS OF DEVELOPMENT

It has been observed that the growth and development in various aspects like cognitive, emotional, language, motor, physical and social is inter-related and interdependent. Development in one aspect of the child leads to the development in other aspects as well. As observed by *Pestalozzi*, "Education is the natural, harmonious and progressive development of man's innate powers". *Gandhiji* wrote: "By education, I mean an all-round drawing out of the best in child and man—body, mind and spirit". Education, therefore, has to develop all these in such a way that the development is balanced and harmonious. While taking measures for the all-round development, it must be remembered that all the aspects of development are inter-related and interdependent.

An individual is one 'whole'. He cannot be compartmentalised. All parts of the individual need equal attention. It is very difficult to decide whether it is the hand or the head or any other part which needs more attention at the cost of the other.

Interrelationships of Physical Development and Other Aspects of Development

'Healthy mind in a healthy body' is an old adage and it is true to the core. Appropriate physical development makes valuable contribution to other aspects of development. When a child is physically weak, he cannot devote necessary attention to the cognitive aspect. A physically weak individual may remain emotionally disturbed. Likewise he may not be able to participate in social interactions. His language and motor development may also suffer. A physically unhealthy person, other things being equal, is unable to perform effectively his duties to himself, to the community and to the God. He cannot offer his prayer properly.

Interrelationship of Emotional Development and Physical Development and Other Aspects of Development

A child under emotional strain is likely to be physically unhealthy and socially inefficient. An emotionally unstable individual is not able to acquire cognitive abilities. His motor development may remain stunted.

Interrelationship and Interdependence of Motor Development with Other Aspects of Development

Motor development is closely related to physical development, creative and productive activities. As observed by A.I. Gates, "The acquisition of motor skills is of value not only from the point of view of the personal satisfactions that accrue from competence in self-help and independence of adult aid, but also from the point of view of good social relations with others".

Interrelationship of Social Development with other Aspects of Development

Social development is dependent upon language development, physical development, cognitive development and motor development. Social development leads to development of other aspects. Likewise if an individual does not mix up with others, he may feel lonely. Loneliness may lead to emotional disturbance which may create difficulties in cognitive and language development.

Interrelationship of Cognitive Development with Other Aspects of Development

Without cognitive development, an individual may remain ignorant and indifferent to other aspects of development. He may be termed as a 'snob'. He may not be able to appreciate and understand social relationships. Undue emphasis on cognitive development may ignore emotional side of an individual's personality. His health may also be adversely affected.

To sum up, for the harmonious and total development of an individual, it is absolutely necessary to pay due attention to each aspect of the development as all aspects are interrelated and interdependent.

Fig. 2.2 illustrates the interdependence of various aspects of development.

Fig. 2.3 illustrates the interrelationship of cognitive development with other aspects of development.

Likewise are the interrelations of other aspects of development.

DIFFERENT STAGES OF DEVELOPMENT AND IMPLICATIONS

Strictly speaking there is no sharp line of demarcation between one stage of growth and development and the other. Nevertheless each stage has certain specific characteristics which must be kept in view while upbringing and teaching children. There is no doubt

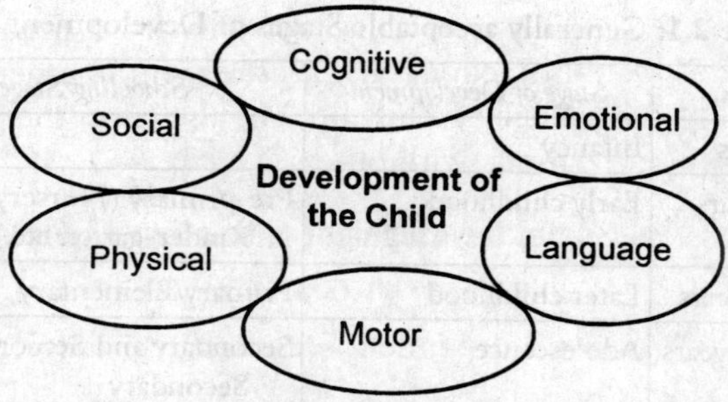

Fig. 2.2: Interdependence of Various Aspects of Development

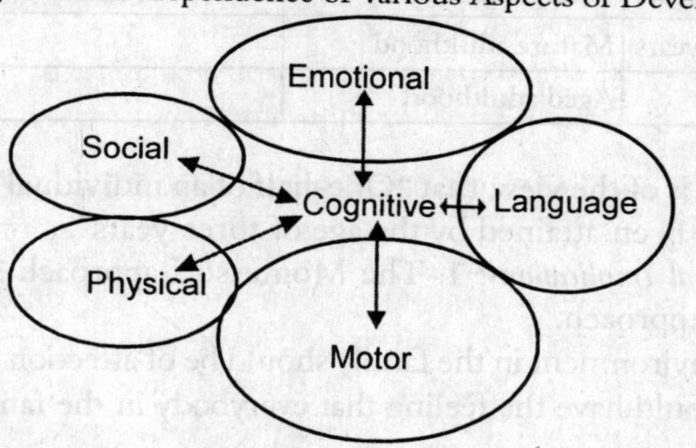

Fig. 2.3: Interrelationship of Cognitive Development with Other Aspects of Developments

that the entire development is usually influenced by two important factors, i.e., (i) Heredity and (ii) Environment. Each stage has its own problems of development.

Scholars and thinkers differ as regards the ages of various stages of development. Here the generally acceptable stages of development are given in Table 2.1.

Infancy (from Birth to 2 years)

Characteristics: The period is marked by rapid physical growth.

Importance: Modern researches have established that the period of infancy is the foundation on which the future development of the child depends.

Highlighting its importance *Ruth Strang* of Columbia University remarked "During the first two years of his life he lays the foundation for his future". *Dr. F. Goodenough*, a prominent child

Table 2.1: Generally acceptable Stages of Development

Age Groups	*Stage of Development*	*Schooling Stage*
Birth to 2 years	Infancy	
2 years to 6 years	Early childhood	Pre-primary (Nursery/ Kinder-garten etc.)
6 years to 14 years	Later childhood	Primary/Elementary
14 years to 18 years	Adolescence	Secondary and Senior Secondary
18 years to 40 years	Young adulthood	
40 years to 65 years	Mature adulthood	
Over 65 years	Aged adulthood	

psychologist is of the view, that "One-half of an individual's mental structure has been attained by the age of three years".

Educational Implications: 1. The Montessori approach seems to be the ideal approach.

2. The environment in the family should be of affection and love. The child should have the feeling that everybody in the family loves him.

3. Freedom should be given to the child in his movements.

Early Childhood (from 2 to 6 Years)

Characteristics: This is the most important and impressionistic period of child's life. He learns his first lesson of citizenship in the home and the school. He develops the instinct of curiosity. He loves make-believe plays.

Educational Implications: This period of a child's life is of great educational significance. It has been correctly held by *Watson* that "the scope and intensity of learning during this period exceeds that of any other period of development". The following points should be kept in view both by parents and teachers while planning the education of the child at this stage.

1. Provision of Healthy Environment.
2. Rational Treatment.
3. Satisfaction of Curiosity.

4. Learning by Doing.
5. Dynamic Methods of Teaching.

Education may be imparted to children with the help of the Montessori Method which is based on sound psychological principles required for this stage.

These methods provide opportunities for the child to develop his five senses as well.

Play-way spirit should permeate all learning activities.

Later Childhood (from 6 to 12 years)

Characteristics: Bodily proportions change. Generally boys are considered superior in games requiring physical strength while girls are superior to boys on the use of fine muscles and in acquiring skills like drawing, painting, sewing etc. According to *Watson*, "A derivative of anger, annoyance becomes more prominent in later childhood. There is rapid intellectual advancement".

Educational Implications: He develops his basic outlook, values and ideas. We, as parents, teachers and social workers have an important role to play.

The school authorities have a special responsibility towards the development of the child.

1. Child's individuality should be respected.
2. It should be kept in mind that each child is unique.
3. Co-curricular activities should be organised.
4. Group competitions may be arranged.
5. Games should be regularly organised.
6. Creative talent should be developed.

Adolescence (from 14 to 18 years)

Chief Characteristics: (i) There is an outburst of various aspects of development; (ii) It is the period of opposite pattern; (iii) It is the period of preparation for living well in society; (iv) The period is marked by far-reaching sex changes.

Educational Implications: (i) Compulsory physical exercises and games; (ii) Monthly health check-up; (iii) Provision of good library; (iv) Organisation of clubs; (v) Guidance services; (vi) Rational approach by the teacher; (vii) Meeting fears of inadequacy; (viii) No discrimination; (ix) Excursions and educational tours.

Significance of the Knowledge of the Growth and Development Process to the Teachers

A knowledge of development patterns at each stage is essential for psychological, practical and scientific reasons. Proper acquaintance with the pattern of human development would enable the teacher to know to a considerable extent at what age what behavioural changes occur and when these patterns are usually replaced by more mature patterns. This is important as too much is expected from students and if they do not show such results, they develop a feeling of inadequacy. A knowledge of development pattern enables the teachers to adjust the teaching-learning process according to the needs and interests of the students. The teachers come to know when students need special guidance.

Deviation from normal behaviour becomes a cause of anxiety for the teachers as when the pattern of development is normal, one stage leads them effectively into the next.

3

Heredity (Nature) and Environment (Nurture): Development and Educational Implications

INTRODUCTION

There are extreme views regarding the influence of heredity and environment on the development of an individual. However, the fact is that the functioning of heredity and environment is similar to that of two eyes, two hands, two feet, two legs, etc. on the development of a person. Each one is complementary and supplementary to the other. Sometimes one plays a more dominant role and the other relatively less. For the balanced and harmonious development of an individual, a balance and harmonious interaction between heredity and environment is essential. Of course, each has its limitations. There is a limit to which each can influence the development of the individual. The role of the home and the school is to ensure that optimum use is made of these limits.

MEANING OF HEREDITY

O.B. Douglas and *B.F. Holland* define heredity as "One's heredity consists of all the structures, physical characteristics, functions or capacities derived from parents, other ancestry or species."

According to *R.S. Woodworth*, "Heredity covers all the factors that are present in the individual when he begins life not at birth, but at the time of conception about nine months before birth."

Every child comes into this world with certain physical and mental characteristics which he got from his parents and ancestors.

He is born with a body and mind which developed from the fertilised ovum. His limbs and organs grow from the same. Some of his mental tendencies are also based on the same. This is all on account of heredity.

It is seen that a cat gives birth to a kitten, a dog to a puppy and a human being to a human being. It is on account of this factor we say that the class of dogs will give birth to puppies or that like begets like. Still, we find a lot of variation among cats or dogs or human beings even if they are born of the same parents. Why does this happen? We shall make a brief study of this phenomenon.

PRINCIPLES OF HEREDITY: HOW HEREDITY OPERATES

1. *Like Tends to Beget Like*: Black-coloured parents generally have black children, tall parents tall children, bright parents bright children and so on. This holds good of all other characteristics and racial differences. "Nature sees to it that each species or genus breeds true to type, save where there are laws governing occasional deviations."

2. *Principle of Variance*: Only certain traits follow hereditary laws. Common observation shows that although like tends to beget like, yet the resemblances of parents and their off-springs are never perfect. Black-eyed children may be born to brown-eyed parents. Even the two twins are not exactly alike.

3. *Principle of Convergence of Two Life Streams*: A portion of inheritance comes from the maternal side and the remaining portion is contributed by the paternal side, i.e., the child's maternal and paternal lines, contribute about fifty per cent each of his inheritance. More specifically, it is generally assumed that 1/2 comes from parents, 1/4 from his grandparents, 1/8 from his great grandparents and so on from all the other more remote ancestors.

4. *Principle of Chance*: Chance plays an important role, making any absolute prediction almost impossible. This is on account of several reasons: (i) The paring of the chromosomes is in the state of flux; (ii) cell to which the set of maternal or paternal chromosomes go during the reduction division; (iii) the particular cell which unites with another in the maternal and paternal lines; (iv) the pattern of genes in any chromosome; (v) genes carried in any particular chromosome; (vi) crossing over of genes from one

paired chromosome to another; (vii) how dominant and recessive traits will be distributed according to the three to one ratio as per Gregor Mendel's Law (1866), especially if there are less than four children in the family and (viii) determination of sex.

5. *Principle of Dominant and Recessive Traits*: Some traits are dominant while others are recessive causing apparent exceptions to the principle of *like produces like*. The union of the best traits of the father with the best traits of the mother produces talented children. Therefore, a talented father or mother must be the offspring of the best combination of the determiners in the germ cells of his or her parents. But such gifted parents may carry on the determiners of genes which are average. There are many chances that when they produce a child, their average traits combine and a child of average calibre may be the result.

CHART SHOWING THE CONTRIBUTION OF HEREDITY ON PERSONALITY DEVELOPMENT

Structural Influences (Tendencies Towards a Structure)	*Behaviour Influences (Tendency to Behave)*
(a) Bodily weight	(1) Nature response (Reacting quickly or slowly)
(b) Bodily structure (Skeletal etc.)	(2) Sensory response (Sense of touch etc.)
(c) Sex	(3) Operation of the Vegetative System (Reproductory System etc.)
(d) Appearance (Skin, colour etc.)	(4) Functioning of the endocrine system
(e) Internal Structure (Size of the heart etc.)	

ENVIRONMENT

Meaning of Environment

In a broad sense, environment means cultural, economic, intellectual, moral, physical, political, religious and social factors which influence the development of the individual. All these factors influence and mould the behaviour of a person from time to time. Two individuals born with the same biological heritage differ because of differing environments. Sometimes it is said that environment is nothing but a process under suitable conditions to change the shape of raw material just as a potter does while making toys of mud. But this analogy is not exactly applicable to a human being who is an animate one. He is not only influenced by the environment but also influences the environment. Environment includes the home, the neighbourhood, the peers, the school and a host of other agencies. No individual is the same at maturity as he was born. The environment changes him. Everything that influences the child apart from himself what he inherits from his parents and ancestors is his environment. In this context we may note the following definitions of environment.

E.G. Boring, H.S. Longeld and *H.P.* define environment as "The environment is everything that affects the individual except his genes."

O.B. Douglas and *B.F. Holland* (1947) define environment as "a word which describes, in the aggregate, all of the extrinsic (external) forces influences and conditions, which affect the life, nature, behaviour and the growth, development and maturation of living organisms."

R.S. Woodworth and *D.G. Marques* (1948) state: "Environment covers all the outside factors that have acted on the individual since he began life."

HEREDITARIANS' ARGUMENTS AND STUDIES

Heredity is All in All: According to *A.E. Wiggam* (quoted by *G.W. Allport*, 1948), "Nearly all the misery and nearly all the happiness in the world are due not to environment. The difference among men are due to differences in the germ cells with which they are born."

Study of Family Histories of Some Famous and Notorious Families:

1. *Francis Galton* (1869), a great hereditarian, studied the family histories of 977 famous persons of various western countries. Almost all of them were discovered to be belonging to great families. The results of the study led him to believe that their greatness was due to their heredity.

2. Later, *Karl Pearson* also made research on the same lines and reached the same conclusions.

3. The most interesting study in this connection is that of a *Jukes family*, quite notorious. The research was conducted by *Dugdale* (1877). *Jukes* was a fisherman. His son happened to marry a woman from a very degenerate family. The study was extended to many generations. According to the report of *Dugdale*, he studied 28,309 individuals of the family. Out of them only 350 men and women were normal. The remaining 92 per cent were all criminals, beggars, paupers, prostitutes or diseased ones.

4. Quite similar to this study is the research of *H.H. Goddard* (1912). He studied a house as notorious as *Kalikak* family. Kalikak was a soldier. He married a feeble-minded woman. Later he married in a good family. 480 individuals descended from his first wife and 496 from the second. Out of all the 480 descendants of the first wife none came to prominence. They were mostly feeble-minded, criminals, sexual perverts and drunkards. Out of the latter one there were many famous doctors, teachers, tradesmen, lawyers and administrators.

Study of Siblings and Twins: Results of such investigations have been given in the earlier part of this chapter.

The Study of Hybrids: The hereditarians say that the hybrids are a clear proof of the importance of heredity. The offspring of a mare, crossed with a donkey, lies in the same parental environment as a normal horse before birth. But the issue is a mule, quite different from horse in every respect and it is never a normal horse. The apparent difference is due to heredity.

CRITICISM OF HEREDITARIANS' POINT OF VIEW

The environmentalists criticise this view. They say that the 977 famous persons of Francis Galton were famous not because they were born of famous parents but because they were provided selected environment by the great families. Similarly, the Jukes and the Kalikaks were degenerated because they had Jukes and Kalikaks around them to breed them. A beggar Juke could not provide good conditions of life to his young ones. A prostitute Juke was a very bad model for her daughter and she was sure to be influenced by her and to be allowed into the valley of sin and darkness. A criminal Kalikak could not protect his children from bad influence while he was shut in jail. The wants and needs of life naturally dragged the innocent children to the same paths which had led the elder Kalikaks to jail. The young Jukes and Kalikaks simply imitated the behaviour of their elders. Their needs were seldom satisfied and they were seldom provided with desirable schooling and guidance. Their degeneration was inevitable.

As regards siblings they say that they too are brought up in the same house under the same roof, in the same circumstances and influences. Therefore, they are apt to be similar to some extent. In the case of identical twins, even, some remarkable differences which occur after separation of a long time, have been quoted.

In the case of hybrids they say that different species combine and therefore the differences are natural.

ENVIRONMENTALISTS' POINT OF VIEW

Environment is All in All: J.B. Watson (1925) considered environment all in all in human development. He wrote: "There is no such thing as inheritance of capacity, talent, temperament, mental constitution and characteristics. There is nothing from within to develop. You do not need anything else in the way of raw material to make a man, be that man a genius, a cultured gentleman, a rowdy or a thug."

SOME STUDIES ON ENVIRONMENT

1. *Wolf Children*: In the early nineteen twenties some hunters found two children from a cave of wolves in a jungle. One of them was about eleven years old and the other about seven. It seemed as if the children had been carried away one by one by the female wolf when they were young babies and instead of being eaten up, they were reared up in the cave. The social environment turned them into wild beasts. They howled and crawled like beasts. They could not stand erect. Their limbs were crooked. But they could crawl very swiftly just like wolves. Their jaws had been deformed and disfigured. They ate raw meat and felt restless in the presence of men. They sipped water.

They were taken to a hospital. After some days a priest took them home. He made great efforts to reclaim them. He taught them how to eat and drink. He trained them in wearing clothes. At first they resisted but after some months they began to wear clothes. He trained them how to walk erect and he succeeded soon. Meanwhile the younger child died. But the behaviour of the elder one was modified and he looked like a human being.

The environmentalists say that it was purely environment that turned the children into beasts and again it was environment which brought them back to human form and behaviour.

2. *Story of Monster*: If the eggs of fish or birds are tempered with during the incubation period monsters are born. If the young fish embryos are placed in an ice-box before their eyes are formed some of the young fish hatched out produce only one eye located in the centre of the forehead. In some experiments the eggs of fish treated with magnesium chloride or electric current are hatched as strikingly different off-springs. The environmentalists say that it is environment that works wonders.

3. *Study of Twins*: Environmentalists also studied the twins. Norman made many studies of this kind. He found that twins reared apart did differ in I.Q., weight and other traits, mental as well as physical.

4. *Bloom's Studies*: F.A. Fredenburg has explained the effect of environment thus, "Obviously, there was no genetically based structure of personality but rather a dynamic formation growing out of environmental influences.

5. *Elkins Study*: Elkins (1959), a historian, sees slavery as exerting a crushing blow upon the personality not dissimilar in its effect from that of the concentration camps of Nazi Germany. He maintains that both were closed systems which produced personality changes in the individual. A high degree of dependence was introduced in both systems. There was a total acceptance of the plantation owner as a father-figure among Negro slaves so much the same way as prisoners of war accepted the Nazi S S guards."

6. *East Tennessee Children's Survey*: Caster Lockceler (1942) compared the intelligence of East Tennessee children over a ten-year period. During this time the schools in the area had improved their circulating libraries, the training of their teachers, the availability of free textbooks and so on. It was found that the average

child had gained ten points in I.Q. or nearly one point per year during the ten-year period.

RELATIVE CONTRIBUTION OF HEREDITY AND ENVIRONMENT ON GROWTH AND DEVELOPMENT

Heredity in the Environment

In the words of H.J. Butchar (1968), "It should be realised at once that hardly any observable quality, physical or mental, can be ascribed to the influence of heredity alone or environment alone. Even where a particular observable aspect of behaviour has been shown to be directly influenced by a gene or a single genetic unit (such cases are rare in the study of human beings), this is no guarantee in itself that the observable is not also substantially dependent on variations in the environment. This principle is illustrated by a finding of Hogben about the fly Drosophila, in which he established that "two distinct genetics mutations affect the number of facets in the fly's eye."

According to T.P. Nunn, "The fundamental truth is that it (the child) is a centre of creative energy which uses endowment and environment as its medium; so that the elements it receives from nature and nurture do not themselves make it what it is, except insofar as they are the basis of the free activity which is the essential fact of its existence."

The much-mentioned slogan 'heredity *versus* environment' is misconception. We should talk of 'heredity in the environment'. Both heredity and environment are essential for development. Hence any trait of the individual is the 'product' of heredity and environment. The individual does not equal heredity + environment but equals heredity × environment, i.e., O (Organism or individual) = H (Heredity) × E (Environment). Heredity sets the probable biological limit, whereas environment determines the level up to which the development is possible. Every development is due to an interaction of heredity and environment.

Personality may be compared to a rectangle. Heredity makes the base while environment the altitude. A rectangle cannot exist without either of the two.

Environment Personality Personality Environment

Heredity Heredity

Personality = Heredity × Environment

Sometimes heredity plays a major role in the development of personality and sometimes environment. However, both play their roles. In case both the base, i.e., the heredity and the altitude, i.e., the environment are inferior, we shall have Jukes and Kalikaks as off-springs. (Anti-social and misfit individuals)

INFLUENCE OF HEREDITY AND ENVIRONMENT

	Heredity	*Environment*
1. *In the area of physical growth and development*	Height, bodily frames and structure of the bodily organs are probably determined by the growth potentials in the genes; the structure of the nervous system also is probably determined genetically. The limits of sensorimotor deve-lopment are set genetically, and these limits vary widely. Thus, the great differences in the motor skills and athletic abilities of children, youth and adults are caused, largely by heredity.	All hereditary influences can be distorted by abnor-mal environment. However, physical health and survival itself depends on good care. Good medical skills, including public health practices, and good nutrition are essential. Deficiencies and deprivation inflict huge penalties on the human body.
2. *In mental growth and development*	The evidence indicates that children are born with a very wide range of general mental potential and with different potentialities for music, painting, the other arts, public speaking, and so forth, for which limits are set genetically.	Good environments are needed for developing abilities to levels close to capacity levels.

(*Contd.*)

	Heredity	*Environment*
3. *In mental and emotional health and personality*	People seem to be born with physical structures—nervous system, glands and organs on which emotional stability depends, and they differ greatly in their potential stability as a result; that is some people are much more disposed by heredity to mental instability than others.	If children are raised in a healthful home where the blood or foster parents live in love and harmony and are kind and supportive to the children, there is a high probability that the children will have good mental and emotional health and thus good personality develop-ment. In protective environ-ments, fewer in the population will become mentally and emotionally ill than in severe and insulting environment.
4. *In attitudes, beliefs and values*	Position in life depends a great deal on capacities, which are set, to a considerable extent by inheritance.	Attitudes, beliefs, and values develop largely from the culture in which one is born, and are influenced greatly by ego, or personal involvement.

EDUCATIONAL IMPLICATIONS OF THE ROLE OF HEREDITY AND ENVIRONMENT

The problem is very important for education. If heredity is everything, if we get a ready-made personality by birth and it is to develop according to its own inborn tendencies which are already there in the little child and if all the influences of environment are meaningless, then why to establish so many schools and other institutions for the reform and guidance of children. On the other hand, if it is all nurture that is to count, then why should we tolerate anybody less than Gandhi or Nehru in calibre. In the words of *Woodworth*: "Shall the gardener pin his hope on careful cultivation of the soil or on selection of the best seed?" Both the schools have their own claims and arguments. Let us discuss the same.

The parents, the teachers and the community have to play a significant role in providing rich environment in all its facets. As teachers we have to have a greater faith in the force of environment though the force of heredity cannot be totally ignored. Education can eliminate those influences and circumstances which inhibit and stunt the full growth and development of inherited traits and capacities and encourage and provide for those which favour it. Scientific educational principles require that the inherited inclinations, capacities and interests of every child should be studied early and every facility should be provided in the environment to develop all that is best in him as an individual. Educational institutions should provide suitable opportunities for every individual to unfold his latent powers. A rich and fruitful environment must be provided to draw out the best in child and man—body, mind and soul. Individual differences of children must be found out and necessary conditions created for their optimum development.

4

Individual Differences: Types and Educational Implications

SIGNIFICANCE OF INDIVIDUAL DIFFERENCES AMONG CHILDREN

Teaching-learning process to be effective and inspirational must take into consideration the individual differences of the learners. The focus should be on the ability of the learners. There cannot be child-centred education without realising the differences and similarities among learners. At the same time, it must be appreciated that there cannot be, in general, individualised instruction in normal schools of the formal system of education. In Chapters 10 and 15, we have discussed teaching-learning strategies relating to learner centred techniques of exceptional children. In this chapter we are primarily concerned with individual differences in general and their classroom implications.

The following description of individual differences has been very beautifully given by Rita Malhotra, Director of a Guidance Centre in New Delhi in '*Journal of Indian Education*' (Volume XXII, February 2002, No. 4).

"Millions and millions of persons have been born and have died.

But no two persons were identical.

Billions and billions of persons will be born and will die.

But no two persons will be identical.

Trillions and trillions of leaves grow and fade away.

But no two leaves are identical.

Nature is perfectly imperfect.

Universe is designed to coexist with imperfections and individual differences."

This description equally applies to individual differences of learners.

Individual differences play the most dominating role in the development of the individuality of the child. It is of utmost importance to study the significances of individual differences.

H.C. Mckown has given a very vivid description of individual differences, "In the whole world there are probably no two things alike—no two trees, no two leaves, flowers, blades of grass, rocks, drops, clouds, animals, houses, pianos, books, baseballs or photographs, even though at first glance they appear to be identical. Similarly no two human beings are alike, they differ physically in size, weight, height, colour of eyes and hair, texture of skin—and in a thousand other details as well as in thousands of details of mental, social and spiritual life". Not only this, an individual reacts to the same situation in different manners at different times. Mass procedures, no matter, how well-intentioned, fail to accomplish the desired results in educational programmes, unless they are supplemented by adequate attention to the individual needs of the learner. In the words of Charles E. Skinner, "Today we think of individual differences as including any measurable aspect of the total personality." Differences in children may be slight, moderate or extreme.

TYPES OF INDIVIDUAL DIFFERENCES

Following are the important types of individual differences:

1. *Differences in Physique*: This means tall or short, thin or fat, fair or black, normal or handicapped, etc.
2. *Differences in Health*: It means healthy or ill, weak or strong.
3. *Differences in Intelligence*: Here the range is very wide—from almost nil intelligence to 140 or above. On the basis of one's I.Q., one can be classified to fall in any of the idiot to genius categories.
4. *Differences with Reference to Achievements*: Pupils differ in achievements in school subjects and their efficiency in vocation.
5. *Differences in Affective Factors*: There are differences in attitude towards ideas, subjects, things and people, etc. Likewise differences in interests.

6. *Differences in Motor Ability*: This means control over muscles. The performance of some in some mechanical task is superior and the performance of others is inferior.
7. *Sex Differences*: Sex differences operate in different ways.
8. *Differences with Reference to Learning Ability and Speed of Learning*: This is evident from daily example. Take a classroom. Some boys learn things quickly—other take days to learn it and some do not learn at all.
9. *Differences with Reference to Race and Nationality*: Many studies lead us to conclude that people belonging to different races and nationalities differ in respect of nature, physical and mental traits, interests and personality, etc. It can be intelligence also.
10. *Personality Differences*: Many classifications of personality differences are made. According to Hipprocrates, people are of four types: (a) sanguine, (b) choleric, (c) melancholic, (d) phlegmatic.

    According to Jung, people can be classified into three types: (a) Introverts, (b) Extroverts, (c) Ambiverts.

    Terman has classified people on the basis of intelligence into nine categories—from genius to idiot.
11. *Differences with Respect to Development*: It includes social development, emotional development which includes emotional maturity, emotional stability, etc.

INDIVIDUAL DIFFERENCES: READINESS

On account of differences in ability and in previous experiences all children are not at the same readiness (preparation for action) for learning when they enter school or when they learn a new topic or unit in the same subject or when they are promoted to the next class. This makes difference in the new situation because of differences in basic concept formation and the level of knowledge required as foundation on which to build a new lesson.

Thorndike has propounded the Law of Readiness. The law states, "When any conduction unit is not in readiness to conduct, for it to conduct is annoying. When any conduction unit is in readiness to conduct, for it not to do so is annoying."

The law is indicative of learner's state to participate in the learning process. According to Thorndike, readiness is preparation for action. Readiness does not come automatically with maturation. It is a law of preparatory adjustment, not a law about growth. Thorndike termed the neurons and synapses involved in the establishment of a specific bond or connection, a conduction unit. According to this law, for a conduction unit ready to conduct, to do, is satisfying and for it not to do so is annoying.

Educational Implications of Readiness. The teacher should prepare the minds of the students to be ready to accept their knowledge, skill and aptitudes. For this, he should provide suitable opportunities for those experiences in which students can spontaneously participate. In other words, he should arouse their capacity to link the experiences with their everyday life. 'Simple to complex' is the important maxim. Aptitude tests may be given to the students to find out their readiness to learn.

EDUCATIONAL IMPLICATIONS OF INDIVIDUAL DIFFERENCES

Some students go faster than others and such students may be given double promotion or separate streams formed or some additional work given to them so that their progress is not retarded due to slow learners. Similarly, steps will have to be taken to ensure that the slow learners also make satisfactory progress commensurate with their capacity and ability to work.

A deaf, dumb, blind, undersized, oversized, too fat or too lean learner needs guidance in the selection of such a vocation where his physical defect may not be a handicap and he may be able to earn his living in an honourable manner. Such students need special educational courses. Ordinary schools fail to do justice to them.

There are some students whose parents are very dominating with the result that their children develop inferiority complex. Too lenient parents allow their children to be freelancers and such children suffer from other complexes and develop bad habits. Children of the rich and the poor have altogether different situations to be faced with.

The problems are as numerous as the learners.

The programme of guidance is not confined to the selection of subjects, schools, vocations, etc. All children need guidance in every aspect of their harmonious development. They need guidance in fields, such as, recreation, moral and religious, social adjustments, cultural pursuits, physical development, etc.

Democratically, all individuals are equal but physically and psychologically all individuals are unequal and in other words each individual is different from the other. All the same, all are agreed that equal opportunity or equality of opportunity must be provided to every individual for drawing out the best that an individual has so that an individual achieves optimum development. It has been aptly stated by Benjamin S. Bloom, an American educator, "A society which places such great value on education and schooling that it requires the individual to attend school for a long period of time must find the means to make education attractive and meaningful to the individual learner." This implies that education should be individual-centred. But in spite of the loud talk on child-centred or individual-centred education, it is observed that there is very little practical action in this regard.

Undoubtedly, all the students need guidance in one or the other aspect, some need more guidance and others less. Without proper guidance the superior child may go astray, the average one may become backward and the backward may be lost to the society altogether.

MEETING NEEDS OF INDIVIDUAL DIFFERENCES: TEACHING STRATEGIES AND CLASS-ROOM MEASURES

In view of the individual differences, it is quite clear that the same curriculum, same methods of teaching and same discipline and in some cases even the same educational institution will not serve the individual needs of children. Ideally speaking each student needs a particular setting and individual instruction with a lot of group interaction. This, however, is not feasible in normal classroom routine. At the same time individual differences of children must be catered to. There are nine broad areas, in which a lot of work could be done to take into consideration individual differences. These are:

1. Streaming of students, i.e., making ability groups.

2. Curriculum planning, i.e., providing advanced and ordinary curriculum in different disciplines.
3. Disciplinary treatment.
4. Guidance and counselling.
5. Special schools for the handicapped children.
6. Combining individualised, group and class instruction.
7. Using maxims of teaching and mnemonics.
8. Using team teaching.
9. Taking up projects where possible.

GENERAL GUIDELINES FOR MEETING INDIVIDUAL DIFFERENCES

1. Courses should be selective to meet the needs of individual students.
2. Opportunities for acquiring manual and mechanical skills should be provided.
3. A wide range of pupil experiences may be provided in the school.
4. Remedial instruction should be made available to such students who need it.
5. Courses should be organised in such a way as bright pupils can learn at their own speed and slow pupils follow their own speed.
6. Guidance regarding co-curricular activities should be provided.
7. Counselling should be given to students.
8. Assignments should be adapted to the needs of students.
9. Special care should be taken to accept the under-achieving child as a unique individual. His particular needs should be immediately attended to.
10. Efforts may be made to re-establish child's confidence in himself.
11. The teacher should seek the co-operation of other teachers and the parents of the under-achievers.
12. In case of deep-rooted emotional problems which lie at the root of under-achievement, referral may be made to a child guidance clinic after taking the parents into confidence.

13. Students should be taught to recognise their handicaps, and counselled in methods to overcome or compensate for them.
14. Some programme of parents' education may be taken up as many problems of the students result from unsatisfactory home conditions.
15. School programme should take into account the needs of those students who are not likely to go to college and those who would join college.
16. The school programme, administration and management should be made flexible enough to allow for adjustment to individual differences.

SUMMING UP

In the end it must be stressed that there is a limit to which individual differences of students can be accommodated in the normal class-room teaching. This is possible to some extent when the number of students in a particular class or section is small. In larger classes, it is not feasible to meet with all the individual differences. There must be some sort of flexible environment like the Dalton Plan. Additional time, i.e., other than the normal class time schedule is needed to cater to the specific individual learning needs of the students.

5

Physical Development Pattern and Educational Implications

GENERAL PHYSICAL DEVELOPMENT PATTERN

In the words of R.M. Liebbert, Rita Wicks Poulos and Gloria Strauss Marmor: "Viewed in its larger perspective, bodily growth occurs through approximately the first twenty years of life in humans. It is generally felt to be fruitful to divide this overall growth period into three major sub-divisions—infancy and early childhood (up to about the fifth year of life), middle and late childhood (up to about age twelve), and adolescence (up to about age twenty). Growth is more rapid and more likely to show spurts during both the infancy—early childhood period and the adolescent period than during middle childhood".

Although there are wide individual differences among children, yet physical growth and development seems to follow to some extent a general pattern. This general pattern of development and growth may be summarised as under.

1. *Changes in Height and Weight*: The Table 5.1 illustrates increase in height and weight at different ages.

On an average, at birth a baby is about 56 cm. in height and between 4 and 5 kg. in weight, boys being slightly taller and heavier. During the first two years, there is rapid increase in both height and weight. There is a steady and slower growth from the third year till the onset of puberty. By five years the height of the child, approximately increases by 80 per cent and he acquires almost 3½ times his birth weight. During the period of adolescence we again find a sudden increase in both height and weight. Girls reach puberty about a year or two earlier than boys do. Therefore, at the age of 12, they are found slightly taller and heavier than boys. But they are again surpassed by the boys at about the age of 14. By the end of adolescence, the young men are generally higher and heavier than the young women. Generally both men and women get their maximum height and weight up to the end of adolescence. But there is much variation in weight as it is more susceptible to environmental influences. Therefore, it is no surprise to note the sudden increase or decrease in weight in later years after attaining maturity.

Weight of the brain increases rapidly in the early years of life. By the time the child completes the age of four his brain gains almost 80 per cent of its final weight, another 10 per cent being added by the time he completes his eight years. By the 20th year, the brain gains almost all its weight.

2. *Changes in Body Proportions*: There are changes not only in the size of the body of the child but also marked changes in the proportion of the different parts of the body. For instance, the head constitutes about one-fourth of the height of the body at birth. The size of the head is relatively much larger than the arms and legs. As the child grows older, the proportion of the head decreases. By the end of adolescence, head becomes one-eighth of the body. The other parts of the body, legs, arms, etc. also change in proportion.

Table 5.1: Mean Height and Weight of Male and Female Children (All-India)

Age Group	*Mean Height (cm.)*		*Mean Weight (kg.)*	
	Male	*Female*	*Male*	*Female*
3 months	56.2	55.0	4.5	4.2
4-6 months	62.7	60.9	6.7	5.6
7-9 months	64.9	64.4	6.9	6.2
10-12 months	69.5	66.7	7.4	6.6
1 year	73.9	72.5	8.4	7.8
2 years	81.6	80.1	10.1	9.6
3 years	88.8	87.2	11.8	11.2
4 years	96.0	94.5	13.5	12.9
5 years	102.1	101.4	14.8	14.5
6 years	108.5	107.4	16.3	16.0
7 years	113.9	112.8	18.0	17.6
8 years	119.3	118.2	19.7	19.4

(*Contd.*)

Age Group	*Mean Height (cm.)*		*Mean Weight (kg.)*	
	Male	*Female*	*Male*	*Female*
9 years	123.7	122.9	21.5	21.3
10 years	128.4	128.4	23.5	23.6
11 years	133.4	133.6	25.9	26.4
12 years	138.3	139.2	28.5	29.8
13 years	144.6	143.9	32.1	33.3
14 years	150.1	147.5	35.7	36.8
15 years	155.5	149.6	39.6	36.8
16 years	159.5	151.0	43.2	41.1
17 years	161.4	151.5	45.7	42.4
18 years	163.1	151.7	47.4	42.4
19 years	163.5	151.7	48.1	42.4
20 years	164.1	151.7	49.2	43.5

Source: Growth and Physical Development of Children. All India—Indian Council of Medical Research, New Delhi, 1968.

3. *Bones*: Most of the bones at birth are soft. The child's bones contain relatively a great amount of water and smaller quantity of mineral matter than those of an adult. More blood flows through their bones than through the bones of adults. They are, therefore, more pliable.

4. *Teeth*: Teeth begin to appear in a systematic order after the age of six months. On an average, around seven months of age, the first two front teeth in the lower jaw erupt and are followed by four molars, one on both sides of the front teeth on both jaws. By the time the baby is 2 to 2½ years old, it will have twenty teeth. Girls show more advanced teeth growth than the boys, except in the case of wisdom teeth, where boys are usually ahead of the girls.

5. *Nervous System*: There is a marked growth of nervous system during the pre-natal period and the first four years after birth. Before birth, the development primarily consists of increase in the number and size of nerves. After the age of four years, the growth of the nervous system proceeds at a relatively slow rate.

6. *Muscular System*: Muscles at the time of birth are more delicate and less firmly attached to the bones than those of adult muscles. The movements of the muscles are random and uncoordinated.

Gradually muscles get changed in shape, size and composition and become firmer and stronger.

7. *Circulatory and Respiratory System*: In early childhood, lungs as well as heart are very small but gradually they grow in volume and height. The veins and arteries do not follow the same growth pattern as that of the heart and lungs. They grow rapidly prior to adolescence but show little growth during adolescence.

8. *Digestive System*: The young child has a small tubular-shaped stomach as compared with the bag like shape stomach of the adult. A young child needs more feeding in the earlier years.

9. *Lymphatic System*: It is concerned with the elimination of waste and destruction of bacteria in the body. From birth onward this system shows the sign of rapid development until it reaches its maximum between the age of eleven and twelve years. After 12 years of age, it decreases rapidly.

10. *Reproductive System*: The development of sex organs is very slow during early childhood but picks up speed as the child advances towards adolescence.

CHARACTERISTICS OF PHYSICAL DEVELOPMENT PATTERN AND NEEDS OF CHILDREN

A. From 5 to 8 years

Physical Characteristics	*Needs*
1. Average increase in height of about 5 cms.	Adequate sleep for 10 to 12 hours.
2. Girls mature faster than boys.	Frequent periods of rest and recreation.
3. Legs lengthen rapidly.	Active play and large space for play.
4. Nose and throat difficulties are frequent.	Guidance in eating and health protection.
5. Tend to take more food than their stomach can hold.	Preventive measures against childhood diseases like measles.
6. Show resistance taking a bath.	Proper dress according to weather.
7. Average gain in health.	Care of teeth, etc.
8. Gradual improvement in speed, steadiness of movement and accuracy.	Varied play activities.

B. From 9 to 12 years

	Physical Characteristics	*Needs*
1.	Children are extremely active.	Careful eye examination.
2.	Relatively free from disease.	Correction of postures.
3.	Relatively healthy and sturdy.	Frequent change of physical activity.
4.	Choosy about food but eat a great deal.	Independence in caring for physical needs.
5.	Girls increase steadily in physical skills.	Adequate nutrition.
6.	Girls usually have less stamina than boys.	Supervision of strenuous physical activities.
7.	Interested in competitive games which require skill.	do
8.	More easily fatigued after physical activity.	do

C. Physical Development at the Adolescent Stage

(Discussed Separately).

GROWTH AND DEVELOPMENT RATE, GROWTH AND DEVELOPMENT CURVE: CHARACTERISTICS AND STAGES

Growth and development rate is rhythmic and regular. It comes in cycle of waves, "periods" or "phases" of growth. This growth rate is not haphazard and random. According to W.H. Krogman, "The child outgrows in obedience to certain biological laws."

According to studies, there are four distinct periods or phases or rates of growth. Two periods are characterised by slow growth and Development and two by rapid growth and development.

Growth and Development Rate at Different Stages in Different Parts and Organs of the Body: From birth to two years growth rate is rapid. This is followed by a period of slow growth up to the time of puberty or sexual maturity which usually takes place between the eighth and eleven years. Onwards till fifteen or sixteen years, rate of growth is rapid and it is followed by a period of fairly abrupt tapering of the growth up to the time of maturity.

(i) The '*body size*' category which includes the skeleton, muscles and internal organs shows more rapid growth during the infancy—early childhood period, and the adolescent period than during middle childhood.

(ii) The '*lymphatic system*' (thymus, lymph nodes, and intestinal lymphoid mass) reaches an adult level by seven years of age and is even larger during pre-adolescence before it declines.

(iii) Similarly, the '*neural system*' (head, brain and spinal cord) is almost fully developed by the age of six. In contrast, the '*reproductive organs*' grow very slowly until adolescence at which point they undergo rapid growth.

Table 5.2: Rhythmetic Sequence in the Physical Development Pattern

Age	*1-2 years*	*2-11 years*	*12 to 16 years*	*17-18 years*
Rate	Rapid	Slow	Rapid	Slow

The Physical Growth and Development Curve

For weight and height curve reflects a steady increase during childhood. The rate is rapid at first and it slows down.

Physical growth follows a cephalocaudal direction, i.e. the rate of growth is faster at the head in initial stages until this area is well-developed. Growth rate then becomes more rapid towards the lower parts of the body. (*See* Fig. 5.1).

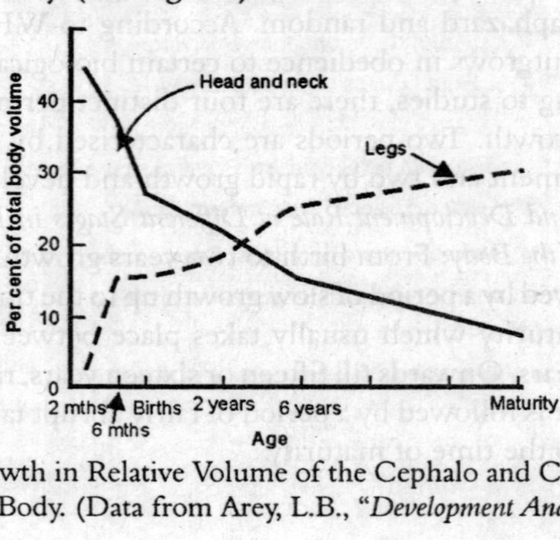

Fig. 5.1: Growth in Relative Volume of the Cephalo and Caudal Parts of the Human Body. (Data from Arey, L.B., "*Development Anatomy*", 1934)

The growth rate of heart beat declines rather sharply during the first two years of postnatal life and then continues a less precipitous decline with further development. (Fig. 5.2).

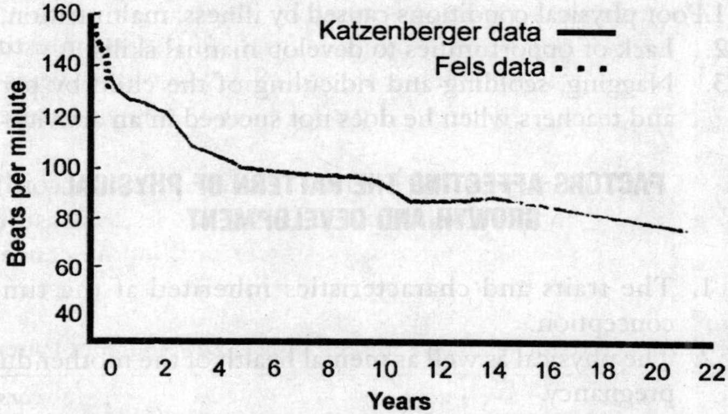

Fig. 5.2: Heart rate at Various Developmental Levels

The general development of motor behaviour is reflected in Fig. 5.3.

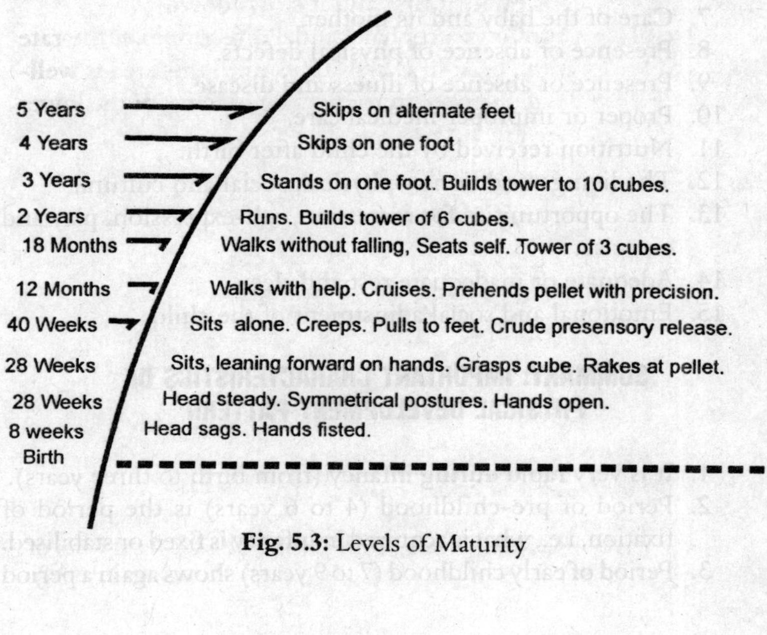

Fig. 5.3: Levels of Maturity

COMMON CAUSES OF DELAYED MOTOR AND PHYSICAL DEVELOPMENT

1. Poor physical conditions caused by illness, malnutrition, etc.
2. Lack of opportunities to develop manual skills.
3. Nagging, scolding and ridiculing of the child by parents and teachers when he does not succeed in an activity.

FACTORS AFFECTING THE PATTERN OF PHYSICAL GROWTH AND DEVELOPMENT

1. The traits and characteristics inherited at the time of conception.
2. The physical as well as mental health of the mother during pregnancy.
3. Nutrition received by the embryo within the womb of the mother.
4. Conditions and care at the time of delivery.
5. Normal or abnormal delivery.
6. Single birth or multiple births.
7. Care of the baby and its mother.
8. Presence or absence of physical defects.
9. Presence or absence of illness and disease.
10. Proper or improper medical care.
11. Nutrition received by the child after birth.
12. The living conditions—physical, social and cultural.
13. The opportunities for recreation, self-expression, play and exercise.
14. Adequate or inadequate rest and sleep.
15. Emotional and social adjustment of the child.

SUMMARY: IMPORTANT CHARACTERISTICS OF PHYSICAL DEVELOPMENT PATTERN

1. It is very rapid during infancy (from birth to three years).
2. Period of pre-childhood (4 to 6 years) is the period of fixation, i.e., what is acquired in infancy is fixed or stabilised.
3. Period of early childhood (7 to 9 years) shows again a period

of growth and development but the speed is slow in comparison to infancy.

4. Later childhood (10 to 12 years) is again a period of fixation.
5. The first three years of adolescence are marked as the years of rapid growth and development. This is followed by a period of slow growth.
6. All the sensory and motor organs of the child's body are in the process of growth.
7. The urge for motor activities like walking, running, jumping, catching, throwing, etc., is at its peak.
8. Muscular development takes place rapidly.
9. In the middle and late childhood, coordination of hands and fingers becomes possible.
10. Children take delight in strenuous physical activities.
11. Children enjoy movement.
12. There is an urge among children to participate in activities which involve speaking, seeing and manipulating.

EDUCATIONAL IMPLICATIONS OF THE PHYSICAL DEVELOPMENT OF THE CHILDREN FOR THE TEACHER

A knowledge of the process of physical development of the children would serve the teacher him in the following ways:

1. The teacher comes to know about the specific needs of children. Consequently he can plan his programmes and help them in their emotional and social adjustments also.
2. Physical welfare of the children is an integral part of the development of the whole child. It is, therefore, very important for the teacher to know the details in this regard.
3. Physical growth and development exercise a great influence on the development of other aspects like intellectual and social development, etc.
4. Knowledge of the pattern of physical growth and development helps the teacher to arrange school programmes like co-curricular activities.

ORGANISATION OF PHYSICAL DEVELOPMENT PROGRAMME

A programme of physical growth and development is not confined to the playground but should pervade the class-room and in fact the entire school programme. Physical development in the class-room may take the following forms:

1. Direct instruction emphasising the necessity of having a good physique.
2. Suggestions regarding the maintenance of good health.
3. Emphasis on right postures.
4. Provision of good seating and lighting arrangements in the class-room.
5. Provision of nutritious diet.
6. Regular medical check-up and follow-up.
7. Free and guided play activities.
8. Activities involving handling of tools and materials.
9. Exercise and morning walk.
10. Yogic exercises.
11. Preparing charts and models.
12. Proper postures.
13. Games and sports.
14. Opportunities of skipping, hopping, jumping, throwing, grasping, etc.
15. Excursions.
16. Community cleanliness programmes.

6

Social Development Pattern and Educational Implications

MEANING OF SOCIAL DEVELOPMENT PATTERN

Social development pattern means the development of an individual in such a way that he becomes an efficient and useful member of the society to which he belongs. He conforms to the culture of the society of which he is a member. An individual, by nature, is a human being who cannot live in isolation. He is compelled by biological, psychological and social needs to live in a group or society. The process of the development of such qualities which bring desirable changes in the social behaviour of an individual is referred to as social development or socialisation of the child.

Important definitions of social development throwing light on its various dimensions are given below:

1. *E.B. Hurlock* notes: "Social development means the attaining of maturity in social setting".
2. *Freeman and Showel* write: "Social development is the process of learning to conform to group standards".
3. *H.E. Garret* is of the view that "Socialisation or social development is the process whereby the biological individual is converted into a human person".
4. *Herbart Sorenson* thinks that, "By social growth and development we mean increasing ability to get along well with oneself and others".
5. *James Drever* states: "Socialisation (social development) is a process by which the individual is adapted to his social environment (by attaining social conformity), and becomes a recognised, cooperating and efficient member of it".

6. *L.D. Crow and A. Crow* write: "Social development means acquisition or the ability to behave in accordance with social expectations".
7. *Freeman and Showel*: Social development is the process by which a person acquires the necessary knowledge, skills and disposition that make him an acceptable member of his own group".

CHARACTERISTICS OF SOCIAL DEVELOPMENT PATTERN

1. Social development begins with the infant's first contact with other people.
2. Social development continues throughout life.
3. Social development is the net result of the child's constant interaction with his social environment.
4. Social development helps in learning and acquiring social qualities of character.
5. Social development enables the child to adjust himself to his social environment and to maintain social relationships.

SOCIAL DEVELOPMENT PATTERN AT VARIOUS STAGES

A. Social Development Pattern or Behaviour of the Pre-School Child

The child at this stage is ready to expand his social contacts. By the age of two years, he can obey certain commands given to him. He calls attention of other persons to objects he feels interested in. He is more or less self-centred. The pre-school child is active. A pre-school child has usually one or two friends. He plays with them only for short intervals. Race, caste, colour or sex or social and economic status have no effect in the selection of friends at this stage. Nursery school experiences contribute in acquiring acceptable social habits.

B. Social Development Pattern or Behaviour of the Primary School Child (6 to 10 years)

By the time a child enters school he wants to have many friends. At this stage he is not satisfied just by the company of his parents. He is interested in the play activities of his group, of the same age and sex. However, quarrels are also common among friends. Boys of this stage tend to be more aggressive. Girls more frequently engage in bickering. Bullying and teasing are more common. Children are interested in group activities and team work. Team games become more interesting than individual work. Social behaviour of the child is greatly influenced by the social environment in which he lives.

C. Social Development Pattern or Behaviour of the Child During the Middle School Stage (10 to 12 years)

1. The period is marked by a greater degree of social awareness.
2. There is a great expansion of child's social world.
3. A child tries to be independent of his parents and other elders.
4. A child becomes an active member of a 'peer group'.
5. There is a sort of segregation among boys and girls of the same age.
6. The child enters the peak of 'gang age'. There is increasing loyalty towards his own gang and conflict with other gangs. The gang life develops many good as well as bad social qualities in the child.

D. Social Development Pattern or Behaviour During Adolescence

(Discussed Separately)

Note: It is not possible to divide the social behaviour pattern at clear-cut stages or ages. Patterns overlap.

Social Development Pattern at Different Ages

Age/Ages	*Social Development Pattern*
First month	A child cannot differentiate between human voices and other voices.
Second month	Begins to recognise the sounds of human being and to give smiles to others.
Third month	Recognises the mother and begins to feel unhappy on separation.
Fourth month	Shows selective attention to the human face and feels happy in company.
Fifth month	Reacts to smiling and scolding. Differentiates between friendly and angry voices.

(*Contd.*)

Age/Ages	*Social Development Pattern*
Sixth month	Recognises familiar faces with a smile and shows definite expression of fear of strangers.
Eighth and ninth month	Attempts to imitate the speech, simple acts and gestures of others.
Tenth to twelfth month	Plays with his image and even kisses it as if it were another person.
At twelfth month	Can refrain from doing things in response to 'no-no' or some other form of request.
One year	Emotional aspects like fear, shyness are seen and social behaviour is linked with these.
1½ years—2 years	Likes to play with toys alone (Solitary social behaviour)
3 to 6 years	Likes to play with others (Social play behaviour), three to six friends. Friends are generally changed.
6 to 8 years	Plays with small groups.
8 to 10 years	Begins to identify the sex difference.
10 to 12 years	Begins to participate in competitive games. Member-ship of friends increases.
Adolescence period	Discussed separately.

FACTORS AFFECTING THE SOCIAL DEVELOPMENT OF THE CHILD

1. *Culture*: A child's social behaviour is regulated by the culture of the society in which he lives. The ways of behaving by the people of one generation, pass on from generation to generation. Our *Sanskaras* shape our outlook and finally personality. There are two ways in which the behaviour patterns of culture are transmitted to the next generation. (a) Directly and formally as in educational programmes at various stages of education, and (b) Informally through interactions between parents and their children which occur in the course of bringing up children. These interactions include the parent's expression of attitudes, beliefs, interests and values, etc. some of the informal social development takes place through interactions with relatives, neighbours, peer groups and teachers and other groups of the society.

2. *The Family*: Among the various social groups, the family makes the first and the most significant influence on the social development of the child. It provides the hereditary transmission of basic potential

for his development. It also provides environmental conditions and personal relationship. Parent-child relations have various dimensions of interaction. As such, they remain basic for social development of the child. Parent-child relationships determine behavioural adjustment of the child in the family.

Religion: Like home, religion has long been regarded as a primary social institution. Earlier religion played a dominant role in the social development of the child.

3. *Peer Groups*: The child is introduced to the social world outside his family, mainly for play purposes. The peer groups satisfy various needs of the children like acceptance, achievement, affection, approval, belongingness, fame, recognition, expression of thought and opinion etc. According to A.T. Jershid (1947), peer association is a meaningful process through which the child changes with his age group into youth and adulthood.

4. *School*: The school life plays an important role in the social development of the child. Its curriculum, co-curricular activities and teacher's influence have a great bearing on the social development of the child.

5. *Community and Neighbourhood*: The environment prevailing in the community has a great influence on the social development of the child.

6. *Mass Media*: Agencies like cinema, newspapers, radio and television, etc., also play a vital role in bringing about social changes in children.

7. *Bodily Structure and Health*: A healthy child has more ability and strength to make himself adjusted in the challenging social setting. A child with poor health or any physical deformity or defect develops feelings of inferiority as well as insecurity in social settings.

8. *Intelligence*: The more intelligent a person is, the more chances of his social adjustment.

9. *Emotional Development*: Emotional development of the child bears a positive correlation with his social development. Emotional adjustability is one of the very important elements of social adjustment.

10. *Physical Health of the Individual*: A healthy child with normal physique is likely to develop more self-confidence than the unhealthy child with not normal physique.

HINDRANCES IN THE SOCIAL DEVELOPMENT OF THE CHILD

1. Social evils like untouchability and caste prejudices, etc.
2. Co-education according to conservative view.
3. Language barriers.
4. Miscellaneous factors like income, occupation and religion of the family.

ROLE OF THE SCHOOL IN THE SOCIAL DEVELOPMENT OF THE CHILD

The role of the school has considerably changed in the rapidly changing civilisations. The traditional role of imparting the basic skills of the three R's is now no longer considered to be adequate to meet the present challenge. The present day school has also to perform some of the functions of the family. It must develop certain desirable moral attitudes and good social habits among students. It is through co-curricular and extra-curricular activities that the task of socialisation can be achieved more successfully. In India today we find that the number of first generation learners in schools and colleges is swelling up. They come from varied backgrounds. Some of them come from deprived homes. It is only the sympathetic understanding and sincere desire of the teacher to act positively in an unprejudicial manner that can help in these situations.

Class in the Process of Social Development

Class provides innumerable opportunities to the children to move and mix with students belonging to different strata of society. This is the beginning of the socialisation of the child for his future life. Here children get many chances to mix without any distinction of caste, colour or creed. The children who are selfish or self-centred learn to adjust their behaviour in terms of class norms. The teachers are expected to be vigilant to ensure that the students do not think in terms of untouchability, caste distinctions and other prejudices.

TEACHER'S ROLE IN THE SOCIAL DEVELOPMENT OF THE CHILD

A teacher's role is very vital in the social development of the child. In recent years, the role of the teacher in functional terms has been gradually decreasing on account of the influence of the electronic and print media. At the pre-school stage and at the elementary stage, teacher's influence on the development of character and personality is of great significance. There is no doubt that, the role of the teachers in the social development of the child is still of great significance.

Following are the important suggestions for the social development of the child which the teachers should always keep in mind:

1. The teachers should demonstrate democratic outlook.
2. Teachers and parents may encourage the children to mix with inter-caste rather than intra-caste and inter-regional rather intra-regional groups.
3. The teachers should respect the personality of children.
4. The mechanism of praise and blame, reward and punishment should be carefully used to socialise the children.
5. The teacher should not show any discrimination. He must ensure a safe and healthy social environment in which the children may imbibe desirable values of freedom, equality, integrity, honesty, patriotism, etc.
6. Community activities like camps, common meals, social service, etc., should be frequently organised.
7. There should be close cooperation between the teachers and parents on matters relating to proper socialisation of the children.
8. Adequate stress may be laid on group activities.
9. Exhibitions on "Know Our Country" may be organised from time to time.
10. Stories depicting self-sacrifice made by great men for the cause of general good may be told to children so that they are motivated to rise above petty gains and work for the betterment of the humanity.
11. With proper guidance and responsibilities, the students' council can build up a sense of shared responsibility among children.

12. Proper socialisation of children very much necessitates that the ideology of the common school system is allowed to function in letter and spirit in India.
13. Children may be taken from time to time to public places like museums, courts, places of historical importance, etc.
14. People engaged in different economic activities or vocations may be invited to school for giving a faithful and pragmatic description of what they do and how useful their work is to the nation. This will enable the children to be acquainted with those around them in the society. This will also develop vocational socialisation in children.
15. Work experience should be introduced in schools. This will enable the children to have first hand experiences of the activities pursued in farms and factories.
16. Children should be acquainted with the social events like the celebration of the birthdays of great personalities.
17. The school or college programme should be full of numerous co-curricular and curricular activities in which children meet, cooperate and learn from each other's personalities.
18. Children should be told about the socially accepted institutions in their society.
19. The introduction of common school dress, common lunch, etc., in the schools and colleges will prevent children of poor and lower middle classes from facing humiliation due to the inflated ego of the children of the well-to-do families who take pleasure in showing off their wealth and status through costly clothes.

CONCLUDING OBSERVATIONS

The task of social development of the child is not an easy one. The educational thinkers point out very emphatically that certain conditions in the learning-teaching situation must be created and made available in the school so that it may become an effective instrument of social development. These conditions are: (i) A democratic social climate in the school; (ii) Effective interpersonal relationships; (iii) Motivated learning situations; (iv) Group methods of teaching; (v) Social discipline; (vi) School-community inter-relationships; (vii) Student participation and involvement in the school management; (viii) A rich programme of co-curricular activities; (ix) Equal treatment to children irrespective of caste or status etc. considerations; (x) Emphasis on egalitarian ideals and values.

7

Emotional Development Pattern and Educational Implications

SIGNIFICANCE OF EMOTIONAL DEVELOPMENT PATTERN

Emotional development pattern plays an important role in the personal and social development of an individual. An individual with stable emotional pattern leads a happy, healthy and peaceful life. He is at ease with himself and his surroundings. On the other hand an individual who is emotionally disturbed becomes a problem for himself as well as for others. Continuous emotional disturbance affects the individual's growth and development. Therefore, the development of emotions is extremely important for the harmonious development of the personality of an individual. Emotions influence all the aspects of an individual's personality. Proper training and education will go a long way to enable the young people to control their emotions and obtain mental balance and stability. Emotions are the prime motive forces of thought and conduct and their control is very important. It has been rightly said, "To keep one's emotions under control and be able to conceal them is considered a mark of strong character".

MEANING OF EMOTIONAL DEVELOPMENT

With a view to understand the meaning of emotional development it is necessary to know the meaning of emotions as they are the prime movers of emotional development.

Etymology: The word emotion is derived from the Latin word '*Emovere*' which means to 'stir up', 'to agitate' or 'to excite'.

Kimbel Young notes: "Emotion is the all-round state of the organism marked by increased bodily activity and strong feelings directed to some subject".

According to *Crow and Crow*, an emotion "is an affective experience that accompanies generalised inner adjustment and mental and psychological stirred up states in the individual, and that shows itself in his own behaviour. By making use of this explanation R.S. Woodworth (1945) has defined emotion in this way. "Emotion is a *moved or stirred up* state of feeling that is the way it appears to the individual himself. It is a disturbed muscular and glandular activity—that is the way it appears to an external observer".

William McDougall (1949) says: "An instinct is an inherited or innate psycho-physical disposition which determines its possessor to perceive and to pay attention to objects of a certain class, to experience an emotional excitement of a particular quality upon perceiving such an object, and to act in regard to it in a particular manner, or, at least, to experience an impulse to such an action". This statement gives us the nature of emotions as well. According to McDougall, an instinctive behaviour has three aspects:

(i) Cognitive or knowing or perceptual aspect.
(ii) Affection or feeling or emotional effect.
(iii) Cognitive or doing or striving or executive, active or behaviour aspect.

Let us take an example. A child sees a bull coming towards him. He experiences an instinctive fear and undergoes the above three processes. Firstly, he perceives the bull, secondly he experiences an emotion of fear and thirdly he tries to run away. It is, therefore, concluded that an emotion is an affective experience that one undergoes during an instinctive excitement.

McDougall discovered 14 basic instincts and pointed out that each and every emotion, whatever it may be, is the product of some instinctive behaviour.

The instincts in their alphabetical order with their associated emotions are listed as under:

Sl. No.	Instinct	Emotion Accompanying an Instinct
1.	Acquisition	Feeling of ownership
2.	Appeal	Distress
3.	Construction	Feeling of creativeness
4.	Curiosity	Wonder
5.	Flight or Escape	Fear
6.	Food seeking	Appetite
7.	Gregariousness	Feeling of loneliness
8.	Laughter	Amusement
9.	Parental	Tenderness, Love
10.	Pugnacity or Combat	Anger
11.	Repulsion	Disgust
12.	Sex mating	Lust
13.	Submission	Negative feeling

CHIEF CHARACTERISTICS OF EMOTIONS

1. The emotional experiences are associated with some instincts or biological drives.
2. Emotions, in general, are the product of perception.
3. The core of an emotion is feeling which is essentially linked with some sort of urge or impulse act to do. There is only a difference of degree between feeling and emotion.
4. Every emotional experience involves several physical and psychological changes in the organism. Some of these changes like the bulge of the eyes, the flush of the face, the flow of tears, the pulse rate, etc., are easily observable. There are also internal physiological changes like circulation of blood, the impact on the digestive system and the changes in the functioning of some glands, etc.
5. Emotions are frequent.
6. Emotions are expressed in relation to the concrete objects or situations.
7. Emotions are temporary.

8. Emotional expressions in early childhood are intense irrespective of the intensity of the stimulus.
9. Small children fail to hide their emotions and express them indirectly through different activities like crying, nail-biting, thumb-sucking and speech difficulties.
10. Emotions are prevalent in every living organism.
11. Emotions are present at all stages of development and can be aroused in young as well as in old.
12. Emotions differ from person to person.
13. Same emotion can be aroused by a number of different stimuli—objects or situations.
14. Emotions rise abruptly but die slowly.
15. Emotions are subject to displacement. The anger aroused on account of one stimuli gets transferred to other situations. The anger caused by the rebuking of the officer to his subordinate may be transferred in beating the children at home.
16. One emotion may give rise to a number of likewise emotions.

POSITIVE AND NEGATIVE EFFECTS OF EMOTIONS

Positive Effects of Emotions

1. Emotions provide energy to an individual to face a particular situation.
2. Emotions work as motivators of our behaviour.
3. Emotions influence our adjustment in the society.

Negative Effects of Emotions

1. Highly emotional conditions disturb the mental equilibrium of an individual.

2. Highly emotional conditions disturb the reasoning and thinking of an individual.

UNDERSTANDING EMOTIONS OF ANGER, FEAR, LOVE AND JEALOUSY

Emotion	*Signs*	*Contributory Factors*	*Values*	*Methods of Dealing*
1. *Anger*	(i) Extreme rage	1. Unnecessary interference in the child's daily affairs	1. Sometimes performance of brave tasks	1. Understanding the causes of anger
	(ii) Resentment			
	(iii) Irritation	2. Assignment of tasks beyond his capacity	2. Development of insight	2. Minimising provocations
	(iv) Feeling of fear, grief, jealousy	3. Imagined or real favouritism shown by parents and teachers	3. Change in the attitude of parents	3. Restraints on the part of elders
				4. Changing the programme
2. *Fear*	(i) Trembling	1. Sight of an abnormal object and animal	1. Safe-guards against harm	1. Narration of examples set by others
	(ii) Crying			
	(iii) Running away	2. Loud sound or flash of light etc.	2. Developing cautious approach	2. Encouraging children to face situations boldly
		3. Strict discipline	3. Hard work	3. Showing love
		4. Unfamiliar persons or things	4. Punctuality	4. Sympathetic approach
		5. Fear of darkness	5. Change in the outlook of elders	5. Appropriate discipline
		6. Fear of being alone		
		7. Fear of ghosts		
		8. Failure in examination or in some important task		

(*Contd.*)

Emotion	Signs	Contributory Factors	Values	Methods of Dealing
3. *Love*	1. Happiness 2. Belongings 3. Feeling of creativeness	1. Caring 2. Protecting 3. Feeling 4. Foundling 5. Smiling	1. Mutual love 2. Admiration 3. Change in the attitude 4. Enthusiasm	1. Feeling of acceptance. Giving suitable tasks
4. *Jealousy*	(i) Kicking (ii) Biting (iii) Pinching (iv) Scratching (v) Bed-wetting (vi) Thumb sucking (vii) Refusal to eat	1. Feeling of getting less attention 2. Conparison with the performance of others.	May lead to hard work	1. Showing affection 2. Fair treatment 3. Avioding undue competition

EMOTIONAL BEHAVIOUR PATTERN AT DIFFERENT STAGES

A. Emotional Behaviour Pattern of the New Born Infant

According to J.B. Watson (1919), the new born infant, displays three primary 'emotion', 'love' in response to strolling, 'fear' in response to loud noises and loss of support and 'anger' in response to physical restraint. Watson believed that all other emotional responses were built upon these primary emotions through the conditioning process.

B. Emotional Development Pattern During Infancy

In the words of Hurlock, "At birth and shortly afterwards, the first sign of emotional behaviour is general excitement to strong stimulation. There are no indications of clearly definite emotional patterns that can be recognised and identified as specific emotional states".

C. Common Emotional Pattern in Babyhood

	Emotion	*Stimuli that Give Rise*	*Response*
1.	Affection	Playing with the baby. Taking care of the baby. Providing toys.	Expresses by hugging and kissing
2.	Anger	(i) Interference with the movements of the baby	1. Screaming
		(ii) Thwarting of some wish	2. Kicking
		(iii) Not being able to do what he sets out to do	3. Waving the arms
3.	Curiosity	Anything new or unusual	Expression of curiosity through facial expression, *i.e.*, opening the mouth
4.	Fear	1. Loud noises	1. Attempting to withdraw
		2. Strange persons	2. Crying
		3. Objects	3. Temporary holding of breath
		4. Dark rooms	4. Stopping the activity
		5. Animals	
5.	Joy	Physical well-being	(i) Smiling (ii) Laughing (iii) Moving arms and legs

D. Common Emotional Pattern During Early Childhood

Emotion	*Stimuli that Give Rise to*	*Response*
1. Anger	Conflict over play things. Thwarting of wishes. Attack from another child.	Temper tantrums. Crying. Screaming. Stamping. Kicking. Jumping up and down. Striking
2. Attention	Loves people, things, pets or objects that give him pleasure	Expresses his affection physically or verbally
3. Curiosity	New things or persons	Sensorimotor exploration. Asking questions
4. Fear	Unpleasant experiences. Frightening scenes on T.V. etc.	Panic, running away, hiding, crying
5. Grief	Loss of something that the child loves	Crying, losing interest in normal activities including eating
6. Jealousy	Parental attitude towards different children, usually new sibling	Open expression, bed-wetting, pretending to be ill showing naughtiness
7. Joy	Physical well-being. Acquiring new objects. Playing pranks with others.	Expression of smile. Clapping hands. Jumping. Hugging the person or object.

E. Emotional Pattern during Late Childhood

According to E.B. Hurlock, following are the chief characteristics of the emotional pattern:

1. Emotional expressions are pleasant ones.
2. The child laughs uproariously.
3. The child displays a release of pent-up animal spirits.
4. Emotional expressions are immature by adult standards.
5. Children who are popular tend to be less anxious and jealous than those who are less popular.
6. In order to win social approval, the child tries to curb the forms of expression that are socially unacceptable.
7. As he grows older, he begins to express his anger through moodiness and sulkiness.
8. Girls are likely to express more fears, worries and feelings of affection than boys.

9. Girls often dissolve expressions of anxiety and fears into tears.

Nevertheless all emotions are not of a pleasant sort. Several outbursts of temper occur.

F. Emotional Pattern During Adolescence

(Discussed Separately).

CLASSIFICATION OF EMOTIONAL PATTERN

1. Aggressive *vs*. Submissive emotional pattern.
2. Normal *vs*. Abnormal emotional pattern.
3. Pleasant *vs*. Unpleasant emotional pattern.
4. Stable *vs*. Unstable emotional pattern.

COMPARISON BETWEEN THE EMOTIONAL PATTERN OF CHILDHOOD AND ADULTHOOD

Childhood	*Adulthood*
1. Too much intensity.	Comparatively less intensity.
2. Short duration of emotions.	Long duration of emotions.
3. Emotions transitory in nature.	Emotions marked by greater degree o stability.
4. Easy detection of emotions.	Difficult to detect emotions.
5. Intensity of feelings rules over reasonning.	Emotional response relatively guided b reason.

Expression of Changes and Emotional Pattern

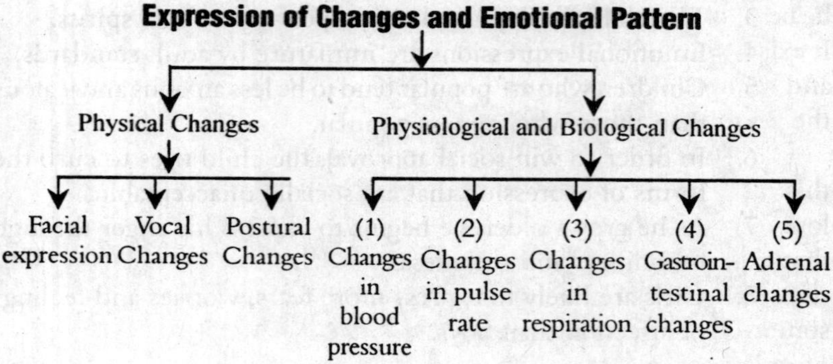

FACTORS AT HOME AND SCHOOL WHICH DISTURB THE EMOTIONAL DEVELOPMENT OF CHILDREN

Some of the important factors which disturb the emotions of children in school are:

1. Lack of security.
2. Economic disparities.
3. Faulty methods of teaching.
4. Fearful atmosphere in school.
5. Emotionally unbalanced teacher.
6. Traditional concept of discipline.
7. Poor physical conditions in schools.
8. Disregard of individual differences.
9. Lack of co-curricular activities.
10. Lack of sex education.
11. Faulty examination system.
12. Faulty curriculum.

TRAINING, SUBLIMATING AND MODIFYING EMOTIONS

1. *Redirection*: An emotion is dynamic in nature and cannot be suppressed totally. It cannot be destroyed. It is just like a tumultuous stream which cannot be obstructed permanently without giving some outlet. But as we can harness a wild stream by building a dam against it and giving new channels to the powerful waters, quite in the same way, emotional waves can also be re-channelled for the advantage of the organism itself and for the whole society to which he belongs. Let us take the example of 'anger'. It is a furious emotion. It exists in its wild form in every organism. We have simply to tame and redirect it to broad and beneficial channels for the benefit of the person and the society.

2. *Sublimation*: Sublimating is also a sort of redirection with this difference only that in the former case the emotion does not lose its original form while in the latter case it is so much elevated that it changes its form. It assumes nobler and higher form. Lust is transformed into love for fine arts or social services or devotion to some deity. *Anger* turns to be *zeal and enthusiasm*. *Fear* takes the form of *anxiety for the betterment* of mankind.

3. *Catharsis*: Intensity of emotions is dangerous for health especially when they do not find expression. Even their expression in original form is very costly for the mind and the body. Therefore, catharsis of pent-up emotions is necessary for the well-being of the organism. Play and extra-curricular activities are very useful devices for this purpose.

4. *Inhibition*: Human life is very complex in the present civilisation. We need to control our emotions at every step. Redirection, sublimation and catharsis are not always possible and at every moment. Often we have suppressed our emotions for a short time or for a long time. It can be done with the help of strong will. But we should know that inhibition should not be permanent and we should give some outlet to the pent-up emotions in some form as soon as possible.

ROLE OF THE SCHOOL AND THE TEACHER IN THE EMOTIONAL DEVELOPMENT OF THE CHILD

School is expected to provide a purified, constructive and creative environment to children and teachers can play an important role in this. A teacher should not merely preach the significance of the emotional control, but he should also teach emotional control by personal example. The teacher should be patient and sympathetic towards the expression of the children's emotions. He should not be harsh, otherwise repression and inhibition would emerge and consequently conflicts would arise which may lead to neurotic and psychotic disorders in the children. He should rather sublimate the emotions of children by presenting suitable opportunities and situations for their healthy expression. Scientific methods of teaching and organisation of co-curricular activities would promote the emotional development of the child in the right direction. Undue reliance on codes of ethics, standards and ideals of society, etc. leads to emotional disturbances in children in the long run, particularly when they find their superior themselves transgressing them. "Example is better than precept" is a famous saying.

Important Ways for the Emotional Development of Children

1. *Providing Emotional Security*: When the child enters the school for the first time he finds quite a new world for him over there. He

was just like a prince in the domain of his home. His likes and dislikes had great significance. He felt himself secure physically as well as emotionally. He had a sense of belongingness and his feeling of self-assertion was also satisfied adequately. But everything is changed in the school. He has little significance and voice in the matters over there to start with. All the other children appear to him well-knit and well-adjusted in their own groups while he stands aloof. Sometimes he is ridiculed by the fellow students. All these things make him very uneasy emotionally. If the teacher is also indifferent to him or he proves to be a bit harsh for him, he loses his emotional balance. The teacher should be very careful of this situation. He should try to make the shift from home to school very agreeable for the newcomers. He should see that the newcomer may not feel the change adversely. There may be a welcome committee comprising some pupils under the guidance of a teacher to help the newcomers in desirable adjustment.

2. *Equal Treatment Irrespective of Income*: Poverty is not a bad thing in itself but sometimes it happens to be the cause of emotional disturbance for some pupils in certain situations. At home the poor child was quite contended and happy in his limited world. But when poor children come across rich ones in the school, they find colossal differences between themselves and their rich classmates as regards their clothes, their modes of life, their meals and pocket allowances. Some of them may develop jealousy, worry and inferiority complex if they cannot make proper adjustment with hard realities. Sometimes the teachers aggravate the situation when they happen to be quite partial and do not treat the poor children at par with the rich ones. Heavy financial demands may also disturb the poor children emotionally as they are often unable to meet the same easily.

The school is responsible to the poor students as much as to the rich ones. Resources of poor students should be studied individually with their education. Simple living should be a guiding principle in all the educational institutions.

3. *Dynamic Methods of Teaching*: Faulty methods of teaching do not develop motivation in the children. Therefore, lessons become a drudgery. The children begin to hate the very process of education. There is always tension in their minds. Learning is no more a joyful activity for them.

The improvement of the methods of teaching can go a long way in bringing back emotional security for many children. Educational work can easily be turned into play and then it will be interesting, joyful and at the same time more instructive.

4. *Role of Love in Schools*: In most of the traditional schools teaching is based on fear. Children know that they will be caned if they are not successful in studies. They get heavy home task which is often impossible to complete without help and guidance which is not always available at home. They sleep at night with the 'dreams of canes'. They wake up in the morning with fear and constant worry. Under such circumstances emotional tranquillity is hardly possible.

There is a famous saying, "Love the child and the child will love you. Hate the child and he will hate you". Love should be the basis of all work.

5. *Balanced Emotional Behaviour of the Teacher*: Some teachers themselves need emotional stability. Emotionally unbalanced teachers prove contagious for the innocent children. They themselves become a prey to inferiority complex, persistent worries or over-excited emotions. They are generally irritable and provocative. For the balanced emotional development of children, teachers themselves should be emotionally developed.

6. *Due Regard to Individual Differences*: All children differ mentally, emotionally and physically. But we provide little individual attention to the children in schools. Some of them are backward in studies, while some of them are very superior. But they are dragged on the same lines. The backward lag behind still more. This leads to emotional disturbance.

7. *Creative and Democratic Concept of Discipline*: Traditional methods of discipline are faulty. Sometimes schools are just like jails and some teachers are like jailors. Such discipline is negative. It may serve the purpose superficially but in reality the things are far from being satisfactory. There should be positive devices of discipline. Discipline should be creative and constructive. Children should be made responsible for handling their own affairs as far as it is possible.

8. *Provision of Co-curricular Activities*: All the children and especially adolescents need provision for the expression of their

pent-up emotions and for redirection of their emotional behaviour. In the absence of such provision, emotional stability is not possible. Various co-curricular activities organised properly can solve this problem quite satisfactorily.

9. *Provision of Sex Education*: During adolescent period lack of information about sex causes emotional disturbance. Teacher should provide necessary information about the sex matters and problems. There should be no shyness and this work should be done seriously.

10. *Continuous and Comprehensive Evaluation*: The present system of examination is faulty. Chance factor counts much in this system. It does not measure the all-round development of the child and causes disturbance. Evaluation should be made continuous and objective.

11. *Healthy Physical Conditions in the Schools*: Poor physical conditions in the school bring fatigue and boredom to the children. They are very soon fed up with the school and its activities. Lack of creational activities is also responsible for emotional disturbance. The school authorities should be careful in this respect also.

12. *Rich and Varied Curriculum*: The curriculum in schools should relate to the real life of children. Learning in schools should be related to the modern needs of children.

Summing up

Whenever, a slight deviation from normal emotional behaviour pattern in children is noticed, steps must be taken to find out the reasons and corrective measures adopted. It must be kept in view that a lot of patience is needed on the part of the teachers in this regard.

8

Cognitive Development Pattern and Educational Implications: Piaget's Theory

MEANING OF COGNITIVE OR MENTAL OR INTELLECTUAL DEVELOPMENT

Cognitive development pattern implies the development of the mental abilities and capacities which help the learner to adjust his behaviour to the ever changing environmental conditions. According to *J.S. Bruner* (1964), "Intellectual development is the capacity to deal with several choices at the same time".

Cognitive development is not merely acquiring knowledge and adding to it. Knowledge must be accompanied by understanding and wisdom otherwise it is barren.

Cognitive development is inherent in the development of those basic skills which help us in getting to know the environment. The formulation of all awareness of the environment rests on the proper development of the five senses, i.e., touch, taste, smell, hearing and sight. While the senses are the 'gateways' to all experiences in the environment, the child learns from these experiences and develops an understanding of the world around him with the assistance of certain skills which are 'observation', 'memory', 'classification', 'sequential thinking', 'reasoning' and 'problem solving'. Thus all these elements help in the development of cognitive behaviour.

PROCESS OF COGNITIVE DEVELOPMENT PATTERN

The process of cognitive development implies the progressive changes in the mental process which go on from birth to death.

Mental process is an activity on the part of the organism which is of a psychological nature or involved in the mind. There are mental tests to evaluate a specific ability or performance. Cognitive development includes various aspects, such as, development of concepts, perception, language, memory, reasoning, thinking, imagination and intelligence.

Various Elements of Cognitive Development

(1) Intelligence and Cognitive Development
(2) Sensation and Perception Pattern
(3) Concept Formation
(4) Language Develop-ment
(5) Memory Develop-ment
(6) Creativity
(7) Problem Solving

1. *Intelligence and Cognitive Development*: The results of intelligence tests show that mental or intellectual growth is rapid in infancy, moderate in childhood and slow in youth.

2. *Sensation and Perception Pattern During Various Stages*: Both sensation and perception are considered important aspects of mental development. The elementary impressions are gathered by sense organs. Impression take the form of perception when they are interpreted and some definite meanings are attached to them.

Through experience, child's sensations become perceptions and he is able to give meaning to it. Child's sensory equipment becomes mature at the age of five. He shows great interest in seeing, hearing, touching, smelling and tasting. However, child's sensations do not automatically assume meaning. During his early childhood, the child is more likely to misrepresent things and objects because of lack of experience. For example, when viewed from a distance, a train may appear to a child as a toy train. But gradually child's perceptions become more and more accurate through right kinds of experiences. By the time a child enters the school, he has gained enough experience. Yet he needs assistance and guidance to improve his ability to perceive by having first hand experiences and observations of objects, persons and situations around him. Gradually he develops a proper perception of space, time, form, movement and distance.

Perception patterns become more organised and refined when an individual passes through the years to his adolescence. Now they tend to become more definite, detailed and rich. At this stage they need not be associated necessarily with objects. They are beginning to be influenced by his beliefs, ideals, opinions, etc.

3. *Concept Formation*: Another important aspect of the child's mental development is the formation of concept. A concept is the generalised meaning that is attached to an object or idea. It is the result of one's perceptual experiences. It involves both discrimination and generalisation. Discrimination begins sometimes after the child tries to generalise his perceptual experiences and he begins to acquire concepts. Experience is an important factor in concept formulation. In the early childhood, a child tries to develop various concepts from the concrete experiences in the form of actual objects.

Normally, concept formation proceeds from concrete to abstract, from vague to clear and from inexact to exact, depending on the type of experiences a child receives. The child has a very poor concept of time. As stated by *Crow and Crow*, "Time as such means little to the young child. He cannot distinguish among 'to-day', 'tomorrow', and 'next week' except as they represent words rather than actual duration of time".

In later years, various experiences provided by reading, lecturing and movies, etc., help in concept formation.

Generally, concepts may be broadened, and developed. They may even take a new shape. Wrong concepts can be altogether abandoned.

Gradually as a result of learning and maturation, child's concepts become clear, definite and specific.

4. *Development of Language*: The development of language contributes to the mental growth and development of the child. Important aspects of language development are speech, vocabulary and length of responses, etc.

5. *Development of Memory*: Memory is also an important element of mental development. There is little memory at birth but it gradually increases with maturation and experience. This has been explained by *Hurlock and Schwartz* in these words: "Memory of an impressionistic kind appears in the first half of the year and instances

of the true remembrance appear by the end of first year. During the first year memory is only aroused by sensory stimuli. With the learning of speech the child is able to remember ideationally by the end of the second year. During the first and second years the memory is stronger for persons and objects than for situation. In pre-childhood from 3 to 6 years, situations become significant factors in the child memory. By 3 years the child can recount the story heard a few days ago and he can also give information about past experiences".

A child has a good memory in the earlier stages but this memory is generally a rote memory. His memorisation is without reasoning. He seldom uses logic and insight in memorisation. A child can cram and reproduce the matter easily. The memory tends to function more logically during later childhood and adolescence. A selection process of remembering and forgetting begins to operate. After that memory tends to decrease.

Memory depends upon person to person. It is generally affected by health and situation of the child. The stimuli which are associated with a kind of memory significantly influence, its remembrances or forgetting.

6. *Creativity*: It may be stressed that creativity is the most single ability which is at the root of human progress. Like many other activities, it can be developed at a young age.

In a general sense, creativity is the ability to think in novel ways which result in some new and original solution.

7. *Problem Solving*: All thinking and reasoning involve meeting difficulties, facing complex situations and finding out solutions. An individual is beset with all these since childhood. Thinking and reasoning powers are used in problem solving and these begin to grow as early as two and a half or three years of age. Gradually the ability to reason grows.

FACTORS AFFECTING COGNITIVE DEVELOPMENT PATTERN

1. *Heredity*: Cognitive development of an individual is greatly affected by the interaction between inherited intelligence and the individual's experience.

2. *Physical Growth*: There is a strong relation between physical growth and cognitive development. A healthy person is likely to have a better intelligence than a person who has a poor physique.

3. *Physical Environment*: Physical environment like fresh air, sufficient light and ample space has a great bearing on cognitive development.

4. *Family Environment*: The kind of discussions held in the family, type of reading material like books and magazines read by the family affect the cognitive development.

5. *Socio-economic Status of the Family*: Parents of high socio-economic group have better access to send their children to good schools.

6. *School Environment*: The methods of teaching, availability of good reading material in the library, attitudes of teachers and school discipline, etc. affect cognitive development.

It is concluded that cognitive development is the result of a large number of factors. It is not an automatic process. It is a gradual and painstaking process.

COGNITIVE DEVELOPMENT CURVE

Learning Curve: It is observed that children are able to learn more difficult things as they grow older (see Fig. 8.1).

Steepness of the cognitive ability curve during middle childhood and adolescence is illustrated in Figures 8.2 and 8.3.

Cognitive Development is indicated by growth in vocabulary (see Fig. 8.4).

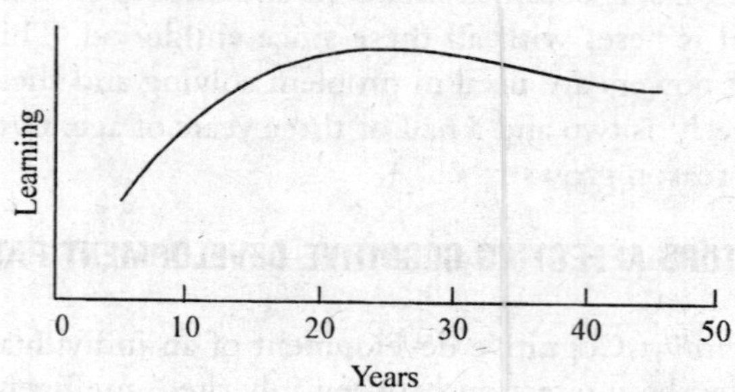

Fig. 8.1: Cognitive Growth Curve (Learning Growth Curve)

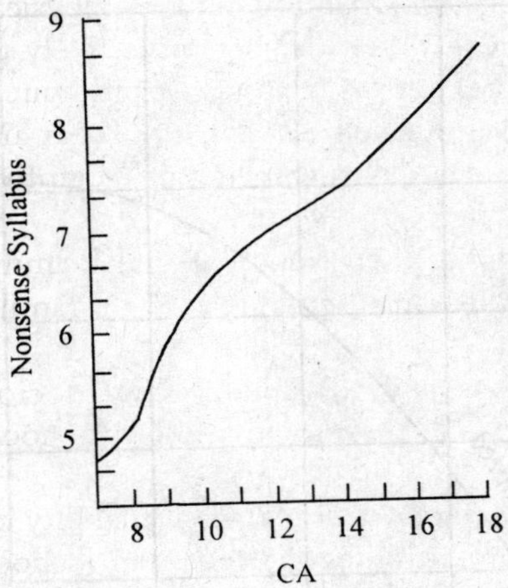

Fig. 8.2: Learning Ability Curve During Middle Childhood

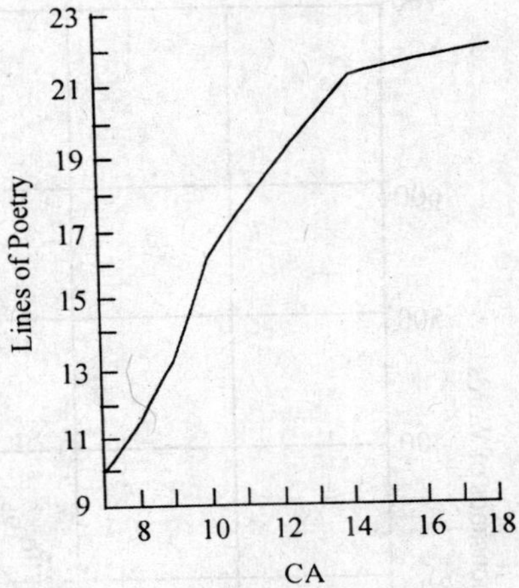

Fig. 8.3: Learning Ability Curve During Adolescence

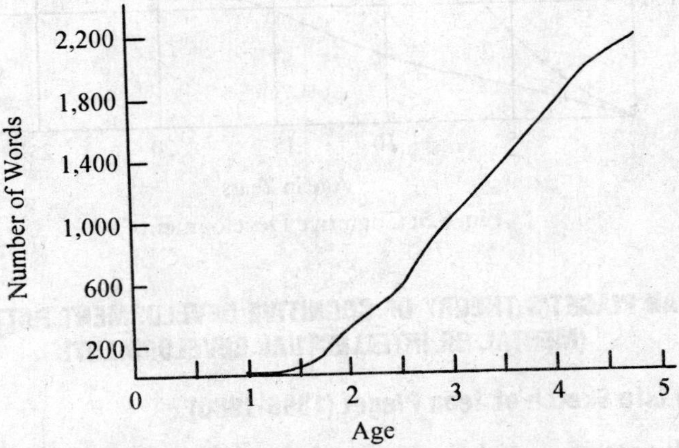

Fig. 8.4: Vocabulary Development Curve During Early Childhood

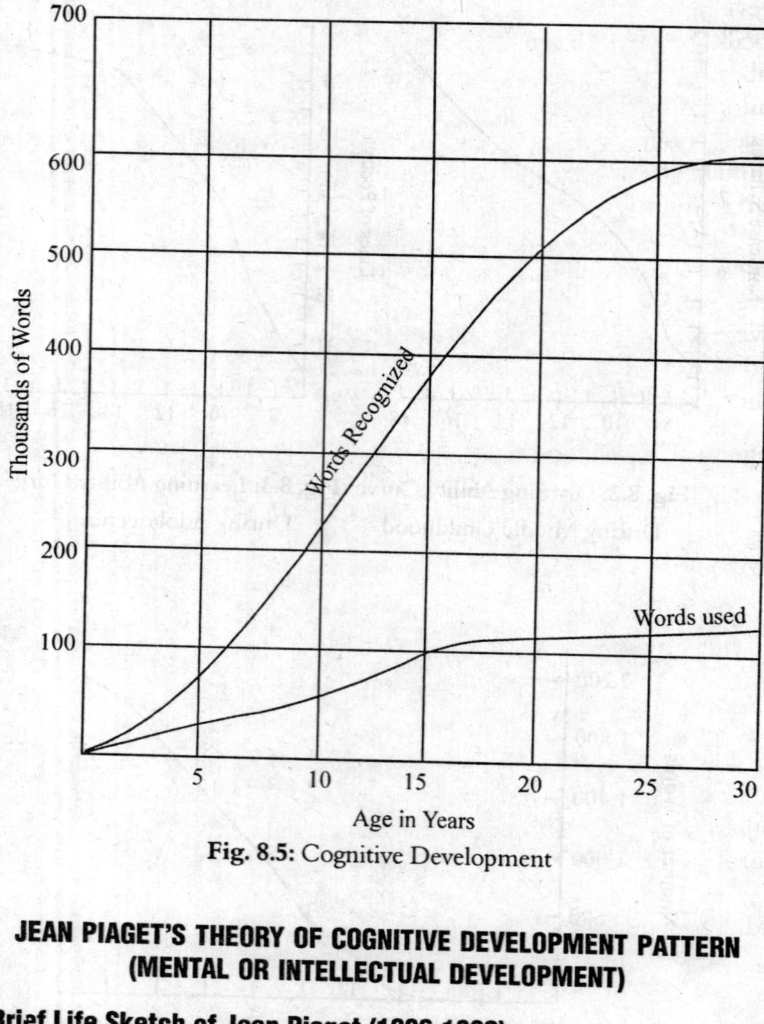

Fig. 8.5: Cognitive Development

JEAN PIAGET'S THEORY OF COGNITIVE DEVELOPMENT PATTERN (MENTAL OR INTELLECTUAL DEVELOPMENT)

Brief Life Sketch of Jean Piaget (1896-1980)

Piaget is regarded as one of the pioneers in psychological investigation of children although he neither undertook formal study nor passed any examination in psychology. He was a biologist by training. At an early age of 22, he obtained his Doctorate Degree in Zoology on Mollusks of Valias. He worked on child development for more than 50 years and produced enormous literature on

Development Psychology. He read Philosophy, Psychology and Sociology etc. He pursued clinical research at the Alfred Binnet Laboratory at Paris. By observing, dissecting and experimenting with children, he developed his educational theory regarding cognitive development or learning by children. His work as a Professor of Child Psychology at the University of Geneva (Switzerland) made him famous throughout the world.

Piaget began his study of child development with the observation of his own three children. From this beginning, his investigations were gradually extended to other children. These investigations resulted in the publication of a large number of papers and books which are often quoted by eminent psychologist and other thinkers on education.

Cognitive Development Pattern at Various Stages

The most detailed description of the development of cognition has been provided by Jean Piaget. Piaget divides cognitive process development into 4 stages or 4 major periods:

(i) Sensorimotor,
(ii) Pre-operational,
(iii) Concrete Operational, and
(iv) Formal Operational.

Piaget asserts that all children progress through all these stages in a fixed order. According to his theory, human intellect is constructed over time as the individual experiences progressively more complex interactions with the environment.

Two Processes: In Piaget's system, two processes—Organisation and Adaptation—actively operate during each of the four stages.

Organisation is the process by which different elements within a system maintain communication, e.g., we have a tendency to organise basic sensory information (such as, images and other experiences) in order to form more complex ideas and thought.

Adaptation consists of complementary processes of assimilation and accommodation. These two processes are the basis for Cognitive Growth.

Assimilation: 'Assimilation' implies incorporation of something from the environment. New ideas, concepts and stimuli are taken in and incorporated into one's 'existing set of schemes'. A scheme is the organised pattern of behaviour which the child develops when he is engaged in any activity. For example, when a child is engaged in sucking, there is a certain pattern of movements of the cheeks, lips and hands. When a child is confronted with a new object, he will try to understand the new object by applying his old scheme to it. He grasps it and adapts himself to a new object by assimilating it. His old scheme does not change in the process.

Accommodation: 'Accommodation' involves modification or change of some elements of an old scheme or learning a new scheme which is more appropriate for the new object. A baby who has already got a scheme of sucking mother's breast accommodates to the object placed in the mouth—finger, nipple, pencil, a toy—depending on its shape, form and the size. The baby develops a new scheme or a modified scheme. This is called 'accommodation'.

Thus a baby assimilates when he understands and perceives the new in the light of his old perceptions. A baby forms a new scheme when he modifies or changes his old perception to suit the new. This implies adjusting or accommodating. In this way a baby forms new structures or new schemes and consequently develops cognivity.

A. Cognitive Development at the Sensorimotor Stage (Birth to Two Years)

There are six steps at this stage.

Step I: During the first month of life, the babies are unaware of themselves and of the object around them, e.g., they do not realise that the bottle they suck and the bottle they grasp are one and the same thing. The infant has a lack of what Piaget calls object permanence.

Step II: During first four months, babies motor activities become more coordinated. They begin to look at the thing which is being grasped.

Step III: Between 4 to 8 months, the infants attempt to control and manipulate the objects which are often conical. They may hear an interesting noise but since they do not know what caused it, they try to make the noise recur by repeating whatever they were doing when they heard the noise. The baby at this stage also realises that objects exist when they are out of sight.

Step IV: During 8 to 12 months, thinking gives way to more instrumental activity. The child has achieved object permanence. He has developed some internal image of the object to help him recall it and its location—he displays sense of space and time—but the child is limited intellectually.

Step V: 12 to 14 months: The child is able to locate the hidden toys. Piaget sees much of the cognitive growth as the formulation of increasingly complex hypotheses in the light of the experiences.

Step VI: 18 to 24 months: During this period the child can infer what the moving hand holds. This last stage is important because it represents the beginning of the child's ability to represent mentally objects that are no longer physically present. In essence, it is the start of abstract thought.

B. Cognitive Development Patterns at the Pre-Operational Stage (2-7 Years)

1. The major advance made during this period is the ability to represent the external world mentally by means of arbitrary symbols that stand for objects.
2. This is the period in which language develops and begins to reflect the child's cognitive abilities and limitations.
3. The pre-operational period is transitional period.
4. The perspective of the child on the world is expanding rapidly, but the child is still confused in the use of physical concepts and in evaluation of cause and effect.
5. During this phase, the child makes appropriate generalisations and attributes his feelings to inanimate objects—assuming, for example, that clouds 'cry' to make rain.
6. Alternate perspectives are not imaged by the child. This is also known as stage of proportional thought.
7. The child cannot do abstract thinking.
8. The child does not think of operations. He is thus a static thinker.
9. The child's thinking is for a very short duration.

C. Cognitive Development Pattern at the Concrete Operational Stage (7-11 Years)

This period (Concrete operational stage) is characterised by the emergence of operations, such as, conservation. Conservation is Piaget's term for the idea that a property or attribute of an object remains the same despite some transformation that changes the appearance of the object. Piaget found that when a child at pre-operational stage is shown two identical balls of clay and then sees one rolled into a saucer he may claim that the saucer contains less clay because it is thinner than the ball. The child is taking only one aspect (shape) into account. The child does not know that this saucer has taken shape from the same ball.

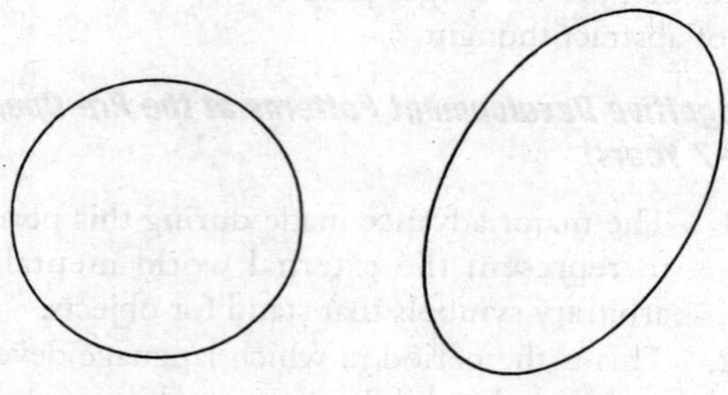

Ball Saucer

At about age 7, the child grasps the solution to conservation problems by developing three concepts that characterise concrete operations. The first is *compensation*—sausage is thinner but that change is balanced by its increase in length. The second is *reversibility*—if you role sausage back, you get the same ball you started with. The third is *identity*—nothing has been added to or subtracted from the clay, so the sausage and the ball contain same amount of clay.

Children at the level of concrete operations are able to consider two aspects of a problem simultaneously. In their social interpretations, they consider not only what they are saying but also listen to others.

The child performs operations: combining, separating, multiplying, repeating, dividing and substituting etc.

He begins to analyse. He is aware of variables. He classifies.

D. Cognitive Development at Formal Operations Stage (11-15 Years or Adulthood)

Here the youth begins and the nature of thought undergoes a change. The complex abstract and mature logic of adult begins to manifest itself during adolescence with the systematic analysis, exploration and solution of problems.

During this period, thinking is purely abstract and hypothetical. Piaget has been most concerned with the capacity to reason with respect to problems, concepts of geometry, language, space, time, number, order etc.

During the teenage years young people realise that thoughts are private and that no one else knows what they are thinking. They value friendship and sincerity and spend much time trying to discern real motives. The adult is more sensitive to the discrepancy between reality and ideals. Teenager has knowledge of the rules and his knowledge is different from that of small children.

Lastly, during this period (Formal operations), the crystallisation of personality development takes place. Forming of social and ideational position is closely linked with the acquisition of moral values.

At this stage, the individual has reached his intellectual maturity.

Problems Related to Cognitive Development

1. Poor environmental stimulation.
2. Poor hereditary environment.
3. Lack of proper attention, assimilation etc. on the part of the learners.
4. Defective teaching-learning material.
5. Low level of learner's intelligence.

EDUCATIONAL IMPLICATIONS OF PIAGET'S THEORY OF COGNITIVE DEVELOPMENT AND THE ROLE OF THE SCHOOL AND TEACHER

1. The child is learning by *himself*, the teacher occupies a secondary position. The child *discovers* things actively. Infants explore the world. Knowledge should not be imposed.
2. It is the duty of the school, teachers and parents to provide materials to children to sharpen their interests. Let the child explore and solve the problems. The classroom in early grades might be arranged in a series of counters stocked with intriguing materials to arouse children's curiosity. Children should be allowed to manipulate things and see results.
3. Instruction should be geared to the level of the child. As the level of the child changes at each stage, the level of instruction or exploratory activities should also change.
4. The knowledge of cognitive stages of growth of a child does help the teacher in more than one way. The teacher should be sensitive to understand the child's actions and be guided by his spontaneous interests.
5. Social interactions have a great educational value for Piaget. Positive social actions, therefore, should be encouraged.
6. Cognitive behaviour skills of the teacher have the following dimensions.
   (a) *Knowledge*: Imparting information.
   (b) *Comprehension*: Making the content clear.
   (c) *Application*: Enabling the learners understand the use of theoretical statements in real situations.
   (d) *Analysis*: Enabling the students to breakdown material into its constituent parts for comparison etc.
   (e) *Synthesis*: Enabling the students to combine elements in components to form new structured wholes.
   (f) *Evaluation*: Enabling the learners to make judgements (quantitative and qualitative) about the extent to which material satisfies criteria.

Following activities should prove useful in developing proper cognitive development pattern:

(i) Story making, telling, writing and listening.

(ii) Picture competition.
(iii) Essay writing involving imagination.
(iv) Assembling of parts of some dismantled object.
(v) Modelling.
(vi) Quiz questions.
(vii) Debates and elocution contests.
(viii) Problem-solving opportunities.

9

Adolescence: Meaning, Characteristics, Problems and Educational Implications

MEANING AND DEFINITION OF ADOLESCENCE

The term adolescence is derived from a Latin word '*adolescence*' meaning 'to grow', 'to mature'. Now this term primarily implies to emerge or to 'achieve identity'. It is very difficult to define exactly the period of life which constitutes adolescence. No sharp chronological boundaries may be fixed to this period. Generally speaking, it covers a period of seven or eight years, normally from 12 to 18 or 20 with large variations in many cases. Some children may manifest traits of its advent as early as the 10th year while others may manifest it till the fifteenth or sixteenth year. Twelve or thirteen may be considered as the normal period for boys in India and even for girls when adolescence begins.

Adolescence is best defined in relation to puberty. This is the period which begins with puberty and ends with the general cessation of physical growth; it emerges from the later childhood stage and merges into adulthood.

According to *G.R. Medinnus and R.C. Johnson*, "Adolescence begins when signs of sexual maturity begin to occur in both physical and social development and ends when the individual has assumed adult roles and is concerned in most ways as an adult by his reference group".

A.T. Jersild observes, "Adolescence is that span of years during which boys and girls move from childhood to adulthood mentally, emotionally, socially and physically".

According to *Dorthy Rogers*, adolescence is "a process rather than a period, a process of achieving the attitudes and beliefs needed for effective participation in society".

The Hadow Report in England has described this stage as, "There is a tide which begins to rise in the veins of youth at the age of eleven or twelve. It is called by the name of adolescence. If the tide can be taken as flood, and a new voyage began in the stream and along the flow of its current, we think it will move on to fortune".

WHO defines adolescence both in terms of age (spanning the ages between 10 and 19 years) and in terms of a phase of life marked by special attributes. These attributes include:

- Rapid physical growth and development
- Physical, social and psychological maturity, but not all at the same time
- Sexual maturity and the onset of sexual activity
- Experimentation
- Development of adult mental processes and adult identity
- Transition from total socio-economic dependence to relative independence

To distinguish adolescents from other similar (and sometimes overlapping) age groupings, which, however, differ in these special characteristics, WHO has also defined youth and young people.

- Youth—persons between 15 and 24 years
- Young people—persons between 10 and 24 years.

GENERAL CHARACTERISTICS OF THE PERIOD OF ADOLESCENCE

1. The adolescent is a combination of opposites. Sometimes he is an altruist and sometimes a miser. On the one hand, he behaves like a child in many ways and on the other hand he likes to be treated as an adult. He wants to have the privileges of adulthood but does not want to undertake its obligations and responsibilities.
2. The adolescent lacks experience though he may exhibit a 'know-it-all' attitude.
3. He regards himself as more suited than the adults and grown-ups to frame rules, laws, codes and morals which will be just and true.

4. He is intensely emotional. He fluctuates between two extremes. He may be active and happy at one time and moody and dull at another.
5. He is seeking his own place in the life around him.
6. There is a strong tendency of self-assertion which is prominent owing to the new orientation which sets in life.
7. The adolescent wants to free himself from bondage. There is a tendency to revolt against authority.
8. The growth of intelligence reaches its maximum during this period.
9. The adolescent is extremely passionate for expressing his own opinions and appreciation.
10. A group of adolescents set to practical work with great zeal and works patiently.
11. He responds more readily to the influence of the teacher than of the parents.
12. There is unlimited admiration for some adult whom he considers to be outstanding. An adolescent is essentially a hero-worshipper.
13. There is lot of interest in and need on physical attractions and good grooming.
14. Girls are more interested in boys than boys are in girls; of course both are interested in the opposite sex.
15. In extreme cases, homosexuality (associated with the same sex) develops.
16. An adolescent exhibits exuberant imagination. This period is characterised as a period of day-dreams.
17. He wants to form small groups or gangs.

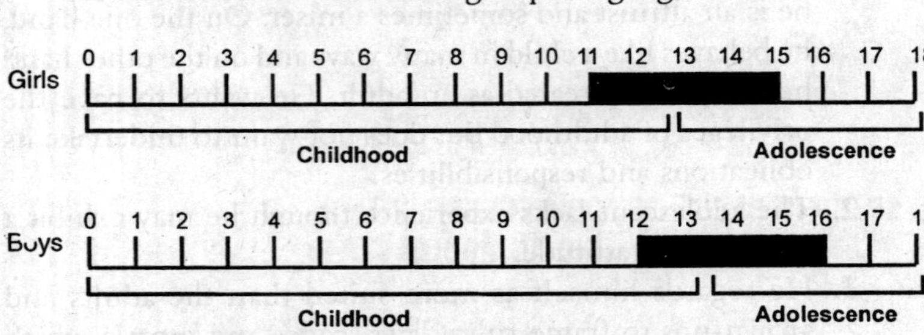

Fig. 9.1: Puberty Overlaps the End of Childhood and the Beginning of Adolsescence

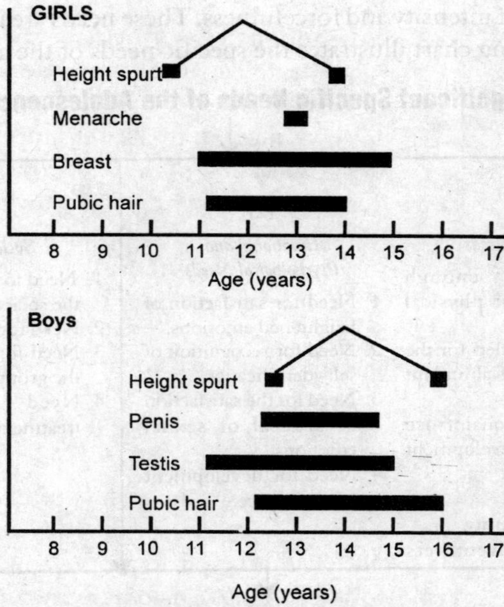

Fig. 9.2: Pattern of Development of Secondary Sex Characteristics in Boys and Girls

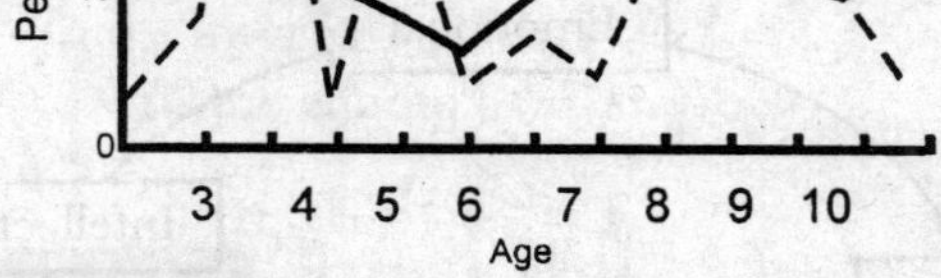

Fig. 9.3: Irritability Tends to Increase Early in Puberty and then to Decline

SPECIFIC NEEDS OF ADOLESCENCE WITH SPECIAL REFERENCE TO INDIAN ADOLESCENTS

Although in many respects, several needs of adolescent stage are similar to the needs of the other stages but they are quite different in the matter of intensity and forcefulness. These needs are interrelated. The following chart illustrates the specific needs of the adolescence.

Significant Specific Needs of the Adolescence

(1)
Physical Needs

1. Need for enough nutrition for physical development.
2. Need for outlets for the utilisation of abundant energy.
3. Need for acquaintance with body development aspects.
4. Need for sex.
5. Need for security.
6. Need for adventurers life.

(2)
Emotional and Psychological Needs

1. Need for satisfaction of heightened emotions.
2. Need for recognition of self-identification.
3. Need for the satisfaction of arousal of sexual emotions.
4. Need for development of confidence.

(5)
Social Needs

1. Need for acceptance in the society.
2. Need for suitable peers.
3. Need for adjustment in the group and society.
4. Need for equal treatment.

(3)
Intellectual Needs

1. Need for the satisfaction of heightened curiosity.
2. Need for independent thinking.

(4)
Moral Needs

1. Need for search for values.
2. Need for equality.
3. Need for sound mind

(6)
Vocational Needs

1. Need for practical experience.
2. Need for appropriate vocational guidance.

The interrelatedness of the various aspects of the development of the personality of the adolescent may be illustrated as under:

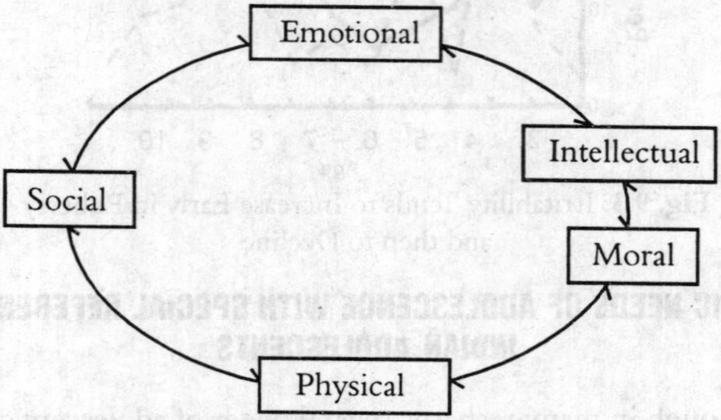

Fig. 9.4: Interrelatedness of the Various Aspects of the Development of the Adolescent

PHYSICAL NEEDS OF THE ADOLESCENTS AND THEIR SATISFACTION

Hall has very emphatically observed, "A ton of knowledge, bought at the expense of an ounce of health which is the most ancient and precious form of wealth and worth costs more than its value". Similar views have been expressed by Carlyle when he writes, "We manufacture clever devils by the thousand because health is not the object of party politics". Great seer Swami Vivekananda has also stressed the importance of well-built bodies when he remarks, "What India needs today is not the Bhagwad Gita but the football field". Our schools must give due importance to this aspect of education. W.M. Ryburn remarked: "We need in Indian Education—a general philosophy of physical education—we need a conception of education in which physical education takes its rightful place and in which its vital importance is recognised".

A properly directed physical development programme should result in health, happiness, efficiency and character.

Meaning of Physical Education and Development

Physical education relating to physical development is that field of education which deals with muscle activities and their related responses. Physical development includes the following aspects:

(i) It is growth of nervous system.
(ii) It is growth of muscles.
(iii) It is functioning of glands.
(iv) It is change in height and weight which people normally observe.
(v) It is development of sex.

Physical development and growth include the physical as well as psycho-motor changes in an individual. Physical development also includes qualities like courage, endurance and self-control.

Physical Development at the Adolescent Stage

At the adolescent stage, marked changes take place in the following domains:

(i) Height and weight.

(ii) Bodily proportions.
(iii) Change in voice.
(iv) Increase in motor performance.
(v) Sexual changes.

Sexual Changes: Sexual changes are very prominent during the period of adolescence.

(A) *Primary Sex Features*

1. Boys develop their sex organs.
2. Sex glands—the gonads—start producing sperms. Boys may suffer from night dreams.
3. The growth of sex glands among girls is not visible. The first menstrual flow is indicative of their sexual growth.

(B) *Secondary Sex Features*

These features are not related to sex organs but are indicative of sexual maturation which is a part of adolescence. These are different in the case of males and females. Among the males the features are:

(a) Growth of pubic hair around the sex organ.
(b) Hair in the armpit, legs, arms and the chest.
(c) The growth of beard, and
(d) The tone of voice deepens.

Among the girls the growth of sex organs is not visible. Other changes are:

(a) The development of breasts.
(b) Increase in the width of hips.
(c) A rounded appearance of body and limbs.
(d) Growth of pubic hair, and
(e) A shrill voice.

Sexual identity includes the expression of sexual needs and feelings and the acceptance or rejection of sex.

Adolescence period is the onset of puberty. Puberty implies a series of physical changes that make the organism capable of reproduction.

Puberty leads to sexual activity, erotic fantasy, experimentation and masturbation.

The period of puberty is a difficult one for most of the adults.

(C) Educational Implications of Physical Growth and Development

A programme of physical growth and development is not confined to the playground but should pervade the classroom and in fact the entire school programme. Physical development in the classroom may take the following forms:

1. Direct instruction emphasising the necessity of having a good physique may be given.
2. Suggestions regarding the maintenance of good health are very helpful.
3. Emphasis on right postures should be laid.
4. Provision of good seating and lighting arrangements in the classroom, thereby impressing upon them the importance of studying under healthy surroundings should be made.
5. Providing ample opportunities to the children for physical activity should be given its due importance.
6. Medical examination of school children by the school doctor should be made at suitable intervals.
7. Physical exercise for every child should be compulsory in the school.
8. Various activities promoting physical development should be well-planned and children should be encouraged to take part in these activities.
9. Activities like woodwork, spinning and weaving, bookbinding, gardening etc. may be introduced in the school as a group project. Such activities will lead to motor development as well as promote cooperation, and emotional adjustment among students.
10. At this stage students also have sexual development. It is necessary for us to impart them sex education.
11. Teachers should be conversant with norms of motor development of the child.
12. A variety of co-curricular activities should be introduced to provide outlets for the development of emotions and instincts which have a close link with physical growth and development.

Summing Up: Montaigne has very aptly remarked, "Physical education does neither train up the soul nor body, but the whole man". Froebel rightly stated, "Early education must deal directly with the physical development and influence the spiritual development through the exercise of senses".

EMOTIONAL DEVELOPMENTAL NEEDS AND THEIR SATISFACTION

Meaning and Need for Emotional Development

Emotional development is one of the major aspects of adolescence growth and development. Not only adolescent's physical growth and development is linked with his emotional make-up but his aesthetic, intellectual, moral and social development is also controlled by his emotional development. To keep one's emotions under control and be able to conceal them is considered a mark of strong and balanced personality. Therefore, adolescents must be trained to control their emotions and achieve a mental balance and stability which will lead to individual happiness and social efficiency.

The term emotion is derived from the Latin word '*emovere*' which means to 'stir', 'to agitate', 'to move' or 'to excite'.

Woodworth, by making use of this explanation has defined emotion in the following way: "Emotion is a 'moved' or 'stirred-up' state of an organism. It is a stirred-up state of feeling that is the way it appears to the individual himself. It is a disturbed muscular and glandular activity—that is the way it appears to an external observer".

Crow and Crow have defined emotion in the following way: An emotion "is an effective experience that accompanies generalised inner adjustment and mental and psychological stirred-up states in the individual, and that shows itself in his overt behaviour."

According to *Kimball Young*, "Emotion is the aroused psychological state of the organism marked by increased bodily activity and strong feelings directed to some subject.

How Emotions Work

All of us observe a large number of persons and objects in the world. We have some feelings for them in our mental make-up. Sometimes our feelings become strong either in favour or against the object or individual or an occasion. This disturbs our mental balance. This disturbance is known as Emotion. It not only disturbs our mind, but the entire organism. It is expressed in various movements and expressions of body and it tries to adjust to face the situation.

Features of Emotions

1. We have emotions due to our intensity of feeling. The depth of intensity differs from individual to individual.
2. The expression of emotions is universal in nature, i.e., it is found in all living beings.
3. Every individual has his own outlet of emotions in his own way.
4. Expressions of emotions are related to a person, object, idea or work.
5. Sometimes the expression of emotions leads to the loss of thinking power.
6. Emotional expression is related to our instinct.
7. Emotions persist for sometime and then they disappear.
8. Expression of emotions leads to changes in our behaviour.
9. Emotions rise abruptly but die slowly.

EDUCATIONAL IMPLICATIONS OF SATISFYING THE EMOTIONAL AND PSYCHOLOGICAL NEEDS OF THE ADOLESCENTS

A suitable educational programme needs to be developed to enable the adolescents to control their emotions and obtain a mental balance and stability which will mark for individual happiness and social efficiency.

Emotions can be suitably modified by the following mechanisms:

(i) Redirection
(ii) Sublimation
(iii) Catharsis
(iv) Inhibition
(Already Discussed)

Factors in School Environment Which Disturb the Emotional Development of the Adolescents

Some of the important factors which disturb the emotions of adolescents in school are:

1. Lack of security.
2. Economic disparities.
3. Faulty methods of teaching.
4. Fearful atmosphere in school.
5. Emotionally unbalanced teacher.
6. Traditionally concept of discipline.
7. Poor physical conditions in schools.
8. Disregard of individual differences.
9. Lack of co-curricular activities.
10. Lack of sex education.
11. Faulty examination system.
12. Faulty curriculum.

Role of the School and the Teacher in Satisfying the Needs of the Emotional Development of the Adolescent

Following are the ways for meeting the needs of the adolescents:

1. Providing equal treatment irrespective of considerations of wealth, status or gender of the adolescents.
2. Using dynamic and progressive methods of teaching-learning.
3. Love and affection on the part of the teacher to be made the basis of work.
4. Balanced emotional behaviour of the teacher himself.
5. Creative and democratic classroom and school discipline.
6. Healthy physical conditions in the school.
7. Due regard to individual differences of the adolescents.
8. Due regard to the individuality of the adolescents.
9. Adequate provision for a variety of co-curricular activities.
10. Provision of sex education.
11. Rich and varied curriculum.

SOCIAL DEVELOPMENT NEEDS OF THE ADOLESCENTS AND THEIR SATISFACTION

Meaning of Social Development

Educators have defined social development in a number of ways.

Freeman and Showel observe, "Social development is the process of learning and conforming to group standards, morals and traditions and becoming imbued with a sense of oneness, inter-communication and co-operation".

H.E. Garret states, "Socialisation or social development is the process whereby the biological individual is converted into a human person".

E.B. Hurlock thinks, "Social development means the attaining of maturity in social relationships".

Herbert Sorenson writes, "By social growth and development we mean increasing ability to get along well with oneself and others".

Thus social development refers to the process of development by which a child acquires the necessary attitudes, skills and values that make him an acceptable member of the group to which he belongs.

Characteristics of Social Development During Adolescence

Following are the important characteristics of social development during adolescence:

1. Adolescence is marked with too much sex consciousness resulting in sexual social relationships.
2. During adolescence loyalty becomes very much pronounced and adolescents are in a mood to sacrifice their selfish interests for the greater cause of the group, society and nation.
3. Adolescence stage is often marked with increased friendly relationships.
4. Emotional behaviour of the adolescent dominates his social characteristics and qualities.
5. There is too much diversity in the adolescents regarding their social interests.

To sum up, we may say that the adolescence is a period of maximum social awareness, increasing and intimate social relationships.

Factors Affecting Social Development of the Adolescents

Important factors are given below:

1. *Personal Factors*: These include: (i) Physical strength and health, (ii) Level of intelligence, (iii) Emotional set up.

2. *Environmental Factors*: These comprise: (1) Family environment, (2) Social and physical environment of the school, (3) Peer group relationships and gang influence, (4) Community environment, (5) Social clubs, (6) Mass media.

According to *T.P. Joseph*, an adolescent wants a friend 'someone to be trusted', 'someone to talk', 'someone who is dependable'.

Harrocks and Benimoff observe regarding the peer influence on the adolescence as, "The peer group is the adolescent's real world, providing him a stage upon which to try himself and others'.

Role of the School in the Social Development or Satisfaction of the Social Needs of the Adolescence

The function of the school has considerably changed in the rapidly changing civilisations. The traditional function of imparting the basic skills of the three R's is now no longer considered to be adequate to meet the present challenge. The present day school has also to perform some of the functions of the family. It must develop certain desirable social habits. It is through co-curricular and extra-curricular activities that the task of social development can be achieved more successfully. It is only the sympathetic understanding and sincere desire of the teacher to act positively in an unprejudicial manner that can help.

Class in the Process of Socialisation: Class provides innumerable opportunities to the adolescents to move and mix with other groups. This is the beginning of the social development of the child. Here children get many chances to mix without any distinction of caste, colour or creed. The teachers are expected to be vigilant to ensure that the students do not think in terms of untouchability, caste distinction and other prejudices.

Role of the Teacher in Social Development of the Adolescent: A teacher can play a vital role in the social development of adolescent under his change. He exerts a great influence upon the development of the personality of the adolescent.

Following are the important suggestions for the social development of the adolescent:

1. Adolescents may be taken from time to time to public places

like museums, courts and places of historical importance etc. to observe social interaction.

2. People engaged in different economic activities or vocations may be invited to school for giving a description of what they do and how useful their work is to the nation. This will enable the adolescents to be acquainted with those around them in the society.
3. Work experience will enable the adolescents to have first hand experiences of the activities pursued in farms and factories.
4. Adolescents should be acquainted with the social events like the celebration of the birthdays of leaders.
5. The school programme should be full of numerous co-curricular and curricular activities in which adolescents meet, cooperate and learn from each other's personality.
6. The introduction of common school dress, common lunch, etc., in the schools will present adolescents of poor and lower middle classes from facing inferiority complex due to the ego of the children of the well-to-do families.
7. Teachers and parents may encourage the adolescent to mix in intercaste and regional groups.
8. The teachers and the parents should respect the personality of adolescents.
9. The mechanism of praise and blame, reward and punishment should be carefully used for the social development of the adolescents.
10. Appropriate social education may be provided to the parents so that they understand the significance of the social development of the adolescents.
11. The teachers should demonstrate democratic outlook.
12. Community activities like camps, common meals, social services etc., should be frequently organised.
13. There should be a close cooperation between the teachers and parents on matters relating to the proper social development of the adolescents.
14. Adequate stress may be laid on group activities.
15. Stories depicting self-sacrifices made by great men for the cause of general good may be told to adolescents so that

they are motivated to rise above petty gains and work for the betterment of the humanity.

16. The teachers should not show any discrimination. They must ensure a safe and healthy social development in which the adolescents may imbibe desirable values of freedom, equality, integrity, honesty, patriotism etc.

Concluding Remarks: The task of social development of the adolescent is not an easy one. The educational thinkers point out very emphatically that certain conditions in the learning-teaching situation must be created and made available in the school so that it may become an effective instrument of social development. These conditions are: (i) A democratic social climate in the school; (ii) Effective interpersonal relationships; (iii) Motivated learning situations; (iv) Group methods of teaching; (v) Social discipline; (vi) School-community inter-relationships; (vii) Student participation and involvement in the school management; (viii) A rich programme of co-curricular activities.

INTELLECTUAL/MENTAL NEEDS OF THE ADOLESCENTS AND THEIR SATISFACTION

Meaning of Intellectual Development: Mental or intellectual development implies the growth and development of those abilities and capacities of the adolescents that enable them to accomplish a task that needs complex cognitive abilities and enable them to adjust their behaviour to the ever changing environmental conditions. Cognitive abilities include abilities like sensation, perception, imagination, memory, reasoning, understanding, generalisation, interpretation, problem-solving and decision-making etc. In fact most parts of the school programmes relate to mental developments.

Main Characteristics of the Mental Development of the Adolescents: The adolescents learn to reason and seek answer to 'how' and 'why' of every thing rationally and scientifically. Power of critical thinking and observation is much developed. They are more creative and inquisitive. They are almost critical of everything. They develop a lot of imagination. This becomes the beginning of the artist, inventor, philosopher, poet and writer etc. in the adolescent. An adolescent tends to become a day-dreamer.

Factors Affecting Intellectual Development: Intellectual development of the adolescent in the school is affected by curricular and co-curricular programme, teaching-learning environment, and the role of the teachers.

Measures for the Satisfaction of Intellectual Needs or Intellectual Development of the Adolescents: Among the important factors are:

(i) Provision of rich curriculum.
(ii) Provision of streaming.
(iii) Provision of varied activities like debates and discussions.
(iv) Provision of socialised teaching.
(v) Project work related to subjects.
(vi) Subject related educational tours.
(vii) Library and reading room facilities.
(viii) Problem solving teaching-learning.
(ix) Challenging questions.
(x) Exploratory activities.

MORAL DEVELOPMENT OR SATISFACTION OF THE MORAL NEEDS OF THE ADOLESCENTS

Meaning of Moral Development: By morality we mean conformity to the moral code of the social group. The term comes from the Latin word '*mores*', meaning manners, customs or folkways. To act in a moral way means to act in conformity to group standards of conduct. Morality also includes a sense of right or wrong—a behaviour which has to do with the conscience of the individual. Moral behaviour is learnt. Moral standards vary from group to group depending upon what has been accepted by the group as the socially approved behaviour. True morality comes from within the individual. It is internal in nature and not imposed by external authority. Immoral behaviour is that behaviour which is unfavourable to the group.

Bowley and others are of the view that a person of moral character has the following qualities: (i) Self-control, (ii) Reliability, (iii) Persistence in action, (iv) Industrious, (v) Feeling of responsibility, (vi) Consciousness.

Several thinkers equate morality with character.

B.N. Jha has stated that character is "a mental factor of the individual, which determines his social behaviour. It is a mental organisation which lies at the back of all his connotations".

A person of character has the following characteristics in his behaviour:

(a) He is firm and not impulsive in his behaviour.
(b) He is not dominated by others in his actions.
(c) He has a strong sense of self-respect and is governed by his self-regarding sentiment.
(d) He is intelligent and cheerful in his behaviour.
(e) He is hard working and faces difficulties with courage and optimism.
(f) He is idealistic in his approach. His inner and outer self is dominated by some ideals.

Most Crucial Areas of Concern: An overview, based on the secondary data available, confirms the need for a separate focus on the health, education, employment and protection of human rights of adolescents. Reproductive health, in particular, represents the most critical area where an emphasis on the special needs and concerns of adolescents is required. In India, given its predominantly patriarchal set up, ideology of son preference, incidence of early marriage and high rates of maternal mortality, a strong focus on the needs of adolescent girls is warranted. However, both sexes are vulnerable to problems such as those of drug abuse, HIV/AIDS and other infections and sexual abuse.

MAJOR INTERESTS, GOALS AND VALUES OF INDIAN ADOLESCENTS

There is a lack of reliable and scientific data on this issue. However, it must be accepted that on account of the influence of electronic media, Indian adolescent cannot remain unaffected by globalisation. Nevertheless, following interests, goals and values of Indian adolescent are discernible although it is very difficult to generalise as there are several sub-groups on account of the vastness of the country and its plural culture.

I. Interests

1. *Recreational Interests*: (i) Interest in folk dance; (ii) Television watching; (iii) Celebrating birthdays and attending parties; (iv) Folk dance and music; (v) Pop dance and singing; (vi) Watching movies; (vii) Reading comics and sensational literature; (viii) Travelling; (ix) Interest in pen-friendship; (x) Interest in television games; (xi) Watching and Listening Cricket commentaries; (xii) Playing cards; (xiii) Trends towards for fun gambling; (xiv) Interest in smoking as a fashion symbol; (xv) Trends towards use of drug and pills; (xvi) Interest in fine arts; (xvii) Exchanging jokes; (xviii) Interest in drinking, it being status symbol.

2. *Religious Interests*: (i) Usually sceptical of religious beliefs; (ii) Disinterest in the observance of religious rites and ceremonies; (iii) In-difference to formal religion.

3. *Social Interest*: (i) Attending group parties; (ii) Mixing with the opposite sex; (iii) Interest in global matters; (iv) Demonstrating self-identity in the group; (v) Group loyalty.

4. *Vocational Interests*: (a) Interest in professions related to Commerce; (b) Interest in information technology and especially computers; (c) Declining.

5. *Miscellaneous Interests*: (i) Conversation in groups; (ii) Interest in beautification of the body; (iii) Interest in new things; (iv) Trend towards foreign studies; (v) Trend towards settling in foreign lands; (vi) Heightened sex interest.

II. Goals

(i) Becoming rich over night, (ii) Getting power and exercising influence, (iii) Capturing political power, (iv) Occupying higher posts, (v) Becoming independent of joint family and having nuclear family.

III. Values

(1) Re-examination of traditional beliefs and customs and acquiring new ones, (2) Emancipation from home and becoming independent, (3) Knowing everything attitude, (4) Growing gulf between the values of parents and adults; (5) Critical attitude, (6) Indifference to respect for elders, (7) Declining faith in the leaders of all shades.

IMPORTANT PROBLEMS AND ISSUES INVOLVED IN THE PROPER DEVELOPMENT OF INDIAN ADOLESCENTS

1. *Serious Problem of 10-14 Year Group*: Since adolescents comprise a major part of the reproductive age group, addressing their needs will be critical in determining India's population. An analysis within the age group itself indicates that proportion of 10-14 year olds is greater than the 15-19 year group.
2. *Problem of Gender Discrimination*: Any programme for adolescents must recognise the problem of gender discrimination of the adolescents.
3. *Problem of Under Nutrition*: If India wishes to achieve the goals of 'Health for All' and adequate 'Nutrition for All', it must attend to the problem of under nutrition among adolescent girls. A sizeable number of adolescent girls are actually malnourished. This will increase the risk of difficulty to child birth.
4. *Problem of Poor Understanding of Reproductive Health*: A poor understanding of reproductive health and sexual issues creates several problems in this area.
5. *Problems of High Level of Pre-marital Sexual Activity, Mainly Among Young Adolescent Males*: In this regard, following trends are noticed:
   - (i) The magnitude of adolescent sexual activity is significant, and is higher in boys than girls. There is also under-reporting of non-marital relationships by adolescent girls due to fear of social disapproval.
   - (ii) Men are more likely to be sexually active and at an earlier age than girls, and attitudes on premarital sexual activity is greater among boys than girls.
   - (iii) Parents and teachers play a minor role in giving information, and are usually reluctant to impart such information. The majority of information on sexual and reproductive issues is obtained from peers (which can sometimes be misleading and inaccurate).
   - (iv) Commercial sex workers usually serve as partners for first-time sexual encounters.

(v) Contraceptive use is low and rarely used in first-time sexual encounters, including with commercial sex workers. Contraceptive awareness is usually about sterilisation, which is unsuitable for most adolescents. Knowledge of HIV/AIDS, safe sex and preventive behaviour (like use of condoms) is low, across all ages and education levels.

(vi) Knowledge of sexual and reproductive issues is extremely poor. In some studies, 50 percent of female adolescents did not know about menstruation, and the limited knowledge was based on social factors (such as, not being permitted to cook) than the actual physiological changes.

(vii) There is considerable interest among adolescent boys for information on reproductive health.

(viii) Education did not increase knowledge of sex and reproduction.

(ix) The educational system does not adequately meet the needs for imparting sex education.

(x) Sexual and reproductive decision-making by adolescents is constrained by age and gender factors. Adolescent women have little choice on whom and when to marry, and are usually not in a position to negotiate contraceptive use. This varies slightly with age, with an older wife more likely to make such decisions.

(xi) There is a huge unmet demand for adolescent health facilities, information and counselling services.

6. *Unwanted Pregnancies and Abortions*: There is a lack of knowledge of appropriate use of contraceptives. Son preference is another reason.
7. *Maternal Mortality*: This is on account of the fact that the body has not yet reached full maturity. Marriage age is very low.
8. *Sexually Transmitted Diseases (STD), including HIV/AIDS*: Young people between the ages of 10 and 25 years make up 50 per cent of all new infections.

9. *Drug Abuse*: In India, it is estimated that a substantial number of drug users are in the age group of 12 to 18.
10. *Violence against Women, Sexual Abuse and Trafficking of Girls*: Available data indicate that a high incidence of rape occurs in the 10-16 year age group.
11. *Gender Difference in Literacy and Education*: The gross enrolment ratio (GER) for girls including adolescent girls lags behind boys. Likewise drop-out rates in the case of adolescent girls are higher than boys.
12. *High Incidence of Unemployment among Adolescents*: Overall, the unemployment rates are almost three times as high for adolescents as that among aged 15 and above.

(*Source*: Adapted from *'Adolescents in India: A Profile'*. UNFPA 2000).

Dr. Tapisha G. Kumar, in a write-up in *'The Hindustan Times'* (Nov-27, 2000) under the caption 'Wonder Years' detailed the following facts regarding Indian adolescents.

1. *Depression Leading to Suicide*: Every year, suicide is one of the most leading causes of death among them. Each year, 15 to 25 per cent of high school students seriously consider taking this course with depression being the prime motive.
2. *Alcohol and Tobacco Abuse*: Alcohol and tobacco abuse is very common among 2.5 to 3 per cent of children between 15 to 20 years of age.
3. *Sex Encounter*: In Delhi alone, 15 per cent of children in the age group 15 to 20 have already had their first sexual encounter.
4. *HIV Infections*: Sex encounter combined with the lack of awareness at this stage has also increased the possibility of HIV (Human Immunodeficiency Virus) infections. India has currently an HIV infection rate of 1.7 per 1000 of which more than 40 per cent is concentrated around teenagers.
5. *Emotional Stress*: Family pressures to study and perform better indirectly result in emotional stress for a teenager.
6. *Improper Company*: Hanging around with improper friends may also lead to drug abuse, HIV and early pregnancy.

7. *Miscellaneous Issues*: Teenagers face numerous issues ranging from pubertal changes, pimples, obesity, short height and changes in body structure, to medical problems like asthma, diabetes, thyroid disorders, eating disorders (anorexia) and bed wetting.

SUGGESTIVE MEASURES FOR MEETING THE NEEDS OF INDIAN ADOLESCENTS

1. *Adolescent Clinic*: Dr. Kumar suggests special adolescent clinics. 'Adolescent medicine' a new branch of medical science, might just be the sweet pill in teen's life'.
2. *National Policy*: There should be a national policy that facilitates establishing adolescent care clinics in hospitals and health centres across the country.

10

Learning: Types and Factors of Learning

MEANING OF LEARNING: DEFINITION, CHARACTERISTICS AND GOALS

Learning is a term used for a relatively permanent change in behaviour or response as a result of practice, training for experience. As a result of learning some change takes place in the individual; now he can do what he could not do earlier. The outcomes of learning from learning activities may be attitudes, skills, social competence and abstract and creating thinking. Learning is an enrichment of experience.

Schools are set up for children and thus learning occupies the central place in the school programme.

Following definitions of learning would help us to have a comprehensive view of learning.

1. For *Boaz*, "Learning is a process by which the individual acquires various habits, knowledge and attitudes that are necessary to meet the demand of life in general."
2. *Commins and Fagin* define learning in these words, "Learning as a sequence of mental events or conditions leading to changes in the learner?"
3. In the words of *Crow and Crow*, "Learning involves the acquisition of habits, knowledge and attitudes."
4. *Encyclopaedia of Educational Research* reads, "Learning refers to the growth of interests, knowledge and skills and to transfer of these to new situations."
5. *Gates* defines learning in these words, "Learning is the modification of behaviour through experience and training."

6. In the views of *Gooch*, "Learning as we measure it is more or less a permanent change in behaviour which occurs under the motivational conditions of practice."
7. In the words of *Hilgard*, "Learning is the process by which an activity originates or is changed through reacting to an encountered situation, provided that the characteristics of the change in activity cannot be explained on the basis of native tendencies, maturation or temporary states of organism."
8. According to *Hunder and Hilgard*, "Learning is the process by which behaviour (in the broader sense) is originated or changed through training procedures (whether in the natural environment or in the laboratory)".
9. According to *Munn*, "To learn is to modify behaviour and experience."
10. *Peal, E.A.* states, "Learning is a change in the individual following upon changes in the environment".
11. *Skinner* views are: "Learning as acquisition and retention."
12. *Travers J.F.* writes, "Learning is a process that results in the modification of behaviour."
13. According to *Wordsworth, R.S.*, "Any activity can be called learning so far as it develops the individual (in any respect, good or bad) and makes his behaviour and experience different from what that would otherwise have been."

Characteristics and Nature of Learning

1. Learning is acquiring new behaviour.
2. Learning is adjustment in behaviour.
3. Learning is change in behaviour.
4. Learning is doing.
5. Learning is a life-long process.
6. Learning is pre-planned.
7. Learning is purposeful.
8. Learning and maturation have positive connection.
9. Learning is related to environment.
10. Learning and intelligence are correlated.
11. Learning exposes 'new vistas' of knowledge.
12. Learning is universal, i.e., both human beings and animals

learn. Of course, human beings have a rational will of their own. They are, thus in a position to get the maximum from the environment.

13. Learning is organising experience.
14. Learning affects the behaviour of the learner.
15. Learning is both individual and social.
16. Learning is affected by physiological, psychological and environmental factors.
17. Learning involves psychological, motor and affective activities.

Goals in Learning: Following are the broad categories:

1. Acquisition of knowledge. This includes (a) Perception, (b) Conception, and (c) Association learning.
2. Acquisition of skills.
3. Acquisition of attitudes, ideals and values.

MAJOR DOMAINS OF LEARNING

There are three major domains of learning as given below:

Domain	*Nature of the Domain*
1. Cognitive Domain	It is related to knowing or intellectual abilities.
2. Affective Domain	It is concerned with emotions, feelings and values
3. Psychomotor Domain	It relates to learning of skills.

Major Areas in the Three Domains

Knowledge Domain	*Affective Domain*	*Psychomotor Domain*
1. Knowledge 2. Comprehension It relates to student's ability of giving: (a) Meaning of a concept, definition or principle	(a) Receiving (b) Responding (c) Valuing (d) Organisation (1) Learning in the affective domain influences attitudes/	(i) Gross body movements (ii) Coordinated movements (iii) Non-verbal communication (iv) Speech behaviour or

(*Contd.*)

Knowledge Domain	*Affective Domain*	*Psychomotor Domain*
(b) Interpretation, i.e., seeing interrelations (c) Extrapolation, i.e., drawing conclusions 3. Application 4. Analysis 5. Synthesis 6. Evaluation The highest form of learning is problem solving. The measurement in the cognitive domain as compared with the affective domain is easy and specific.	feelings and values (2) The measurement of learning in the affective domain as compared with the cognitive domain is less specific and difficult.	(1) Initiation (2) Manipulation (3) Precision (4) Articulation (5) Naturalisation (mechanisation and internalisation). Articu-lation implies coordi-nation of action per-formed with efficiency in terms of time, speed and case. Naturalisation implies per-formance in skill with natural case and almost without conscious effort so that it is like a habit.

LEARNING PROCESS

Aspects of the Learning Process: Learning process in general includes the following:

(i) Acquisition of new experiences.
(ii) Retention of old experiences in the form of impressions, engrams or skills.
(iii) Development and modification of experience.
(iv) Growth and increase in these experiences.
(v) Creation of new experiences.
(vi) Synthesis and organisation of the old and the new experiences, resulting in a novel pattern called learning.

Fagin (1958) states that learning is a sequence of mental events or conditions leading to changes in the learner. As a sequence of events, the learning process is as under:

1. The individual has needs and is therefore in a state of readiness to respond. These are antecedent conditions within the learner.
2. He meets a learning situation or problem. A new interpretation is required because previously learned responses are not adequate for reaching the goal and satisfying his need. He encounters something new or unexpected, and searches for a different response.
3. He interprets the situation with reference to his goals, and tries a response or responses which seem to satisfy his need. The way he perceives the situation and the response he makes depends both on his 'readiness' and on external conditions of the situation.
4. If his response leads to desired goals or satisfaction, he will tend to interpret and respond to similar future situations in the same way. If not, he keeps on trying and reinterpreting until satisfying consequences are attained. The learning process is this whole sequence!

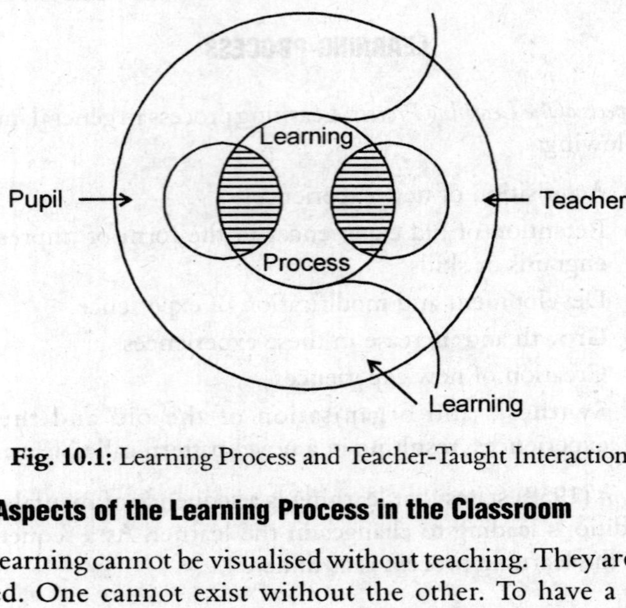

Fig. 10.1: Learning Process and Teacher-Taught Interaction

Four Aspects of the Learning Process in the Classroom

Learning cannot be visualised without teaching. They are interrelated. One cannot exist without the other. To have a proper perspective of the learning process, we must consider it in the teaching-learning situation: teacher, student, learning and the interaction. The teacher creates the learning situation. The process is the interaction between student and teacher. Teaching and learning relationship or interaction may be explained with the help of a diagram.

1. *The Teacher*: The teacher has to be an 'inducer of change'. The teacher has to understand the significance of creating rapport in the class.
2. *The Environment*: The teacher at the very outset must set the stage or environment the effective study of the pupils.
   (i) A definite place of study.
   (ii) Favourable physical conditions for learning such as proper light, adequate space and ventilation, etc.
   (iii) A definite time schedule for study—what to study, when to study and how to study.
   (iv) A clear idea of the purpose of study.
3. *The Child as a Learner*: A wise teacher takes note of the following:
   (i) Individual differences in learning and an individual approach which may, however, differ from child to child or within the same child when his learning takes place under different situations and conditions.
   (ii) Setting up goals or standards not beyond the capacity of the learner.
   (iii) Keeping in view that the previous experience of the learner is fundamental in the process of learning.
   (iv) Awareness of the fact that knowledge of one's own performance, mistakes and information of successful result helps in learning.
   (v) Knowing that the active participation by the learner is essential in learning.
   (vi) Realising that motivation is a powerful influence in determining effective learning.

(vii) Realising that a motivated learner can acquire knowledge and understanding more quickly than one who is not motivated.

(viii) Keeping in view that excessive motivation may sometimes be less effective in some kinds of learning. In some instances it may result in 'pushing' the child too much disregarding his abilities.

(ix) Knowing that learning depends on the mental set or the mood of the learner. The teacher has to find out whether the learner is ready for the task or not. If not, what are the ways and means to make him ready for the purpose.

(x) Believing that emotion of the learner is a powerful factor in learning and the teacher must learn how to use this to his greatest advantage. In this respect the good interpersonal relationships in the classroom as well as in the school should not be neglected by the teachers.

(xi) Having faith that good study habits of the individual also promote learning.

4. *Subject Matter and Its Presentation*: In the course of formal and informal teaching, a resourceful teacher plans and directs pupil experiences which lead to effective learning. The study of the learning process enables the teacher to make the following deductions, with the help of which he tries to affect purposeful learning in pupils.

1. by following certain well-tried principles and maxims of teaching to guide the pupils learning activities;
2. by considering the maturity and the capacity of the learner;
3. by employing fruitful motivational devices;
4. by directing and modifying perception of the learner;
5. by using practices most effectively;
6. by removing emotional disturbances; and
7. by directing teaching towards transfer.

Factors Influencing Learning

Health of the Child	*Personal Factors*	*Environmental Factors*	*Relationships with*	*Media Influence*	*Methods of Learning*	*Methods of Teaching*	*Maxims of Teaching*
(1)	(2)	(3)	(4)	(5)	(6)	(7)	(8)
1. Physical develop-ment 2. Postures 3. General health	1. Sensation and perception 2. Fatigue and boredom 3. Maturation 4. Emotional condition 5. Needs 6. Intelligence 7. Motivation 8. Attention 9. Aptitude 10. Attitude	1. Natural surroundings 2. Social surroundings 3. Cultural surroundings 4. Home environment 5. Class-room environment 6. School environment 7. Political environment	1. Teachers 2. Parents 3. Peers	1. Print Media 2. Non-print Media	1. Whole vs. Part Learning 2. Mediating Method 3. Space vs. Un-spaced Method 4. Recitals 5. Memory Systems 6. Laws of Association	1. Lecturing 2. Demonstration 3. Individual Practical work 4. Individual work in work-shop 5. Field trips 6. Projects 7. Discussion 8. Conference, Seminar etc. 9. Assignments 10. Tutorial (Individual) 11. Programmed Instruction 12. Teaching Machines 13. Electronic Media 14. Audio-visual Aids	1. From known to unknown 2. Easy to difficult 3. Simple to com-pact 4. Concrete to abs-tract 5. Indefinite to de-finite 6. Particular to ge-neral 7. Empirical to ra-tional 8. Deductive-in-ductive 9. Psychological to logical

GENERAL PRINCIPLES OF EFFECTIVE LEARNING

1. Different types of learning experiences should be provided to satisfy the needs of each and every learner as notable 'differences' exist between individuals.
2. Learning experiences should be provided for natural integration of feeling, doing and thinking as the learner is a living 'organism', a unitary integrated whole.
3. Rich learning experiences should be provided to meet the needs of the learner as he always seeks to maintain equilibrium or balance by satisfying his needs.
4. The setting of learning should be purposive or goal-oriented as the learner is a goal seeking organism to satisfy his needs.
5. The learning situations should provide freedom to make creative contribution as the learner is an active, behaving and exploring individual.
6. While providing learning experiences for the learner, family background and individuality of the learner should be taken into account as the learner is a social being and needs social environment.
7. The learner needs sympathy and guidance for his personality development as he is quite immature.
8. Learning activities should be based on cooperative group work so as to develop the socialised personality of the learner.
9. Bright students can learn things quickly than the dull ones.
10. A motivated pupil learns more readily than one who is not motivated.
11. Learning through reward or success motivation is more effective than punishment or failure.
12. Learning goals should be neither too high nor too low.
13. The personality of a teacher is a great contributory factor in teaching-learning.
14. Active participation of the learner is more effective than passive reception.
15. Meaningful materials and meaningful tasks are learned more quickly.
16. Moderate practice and repetition is very useful for durable learning.

17. Effective audio-visual aids contribute to make learning effective and inspirational.
18. Transfer of learning will be better if learner himself discovers relationship between new and old tasks.
19. Optimal learning takes place when appropriate teaching strategies are adopted.

ELEMENTS IN THE TEACHING-LEARNING PROCESS: IMPLICATIONS OF LEARNING FOR THE CLASSROOM TEACHER

The teacher would make learning effective, if he attends to the following elements carefully.

1. *Who is to Learn or Whom to Teach*? The child is to learn and therefore his interests, abilities and aptitudes have to be taken note of. It must be remembered that he is an active being. Individual differences have to be attended to.
2. *Who is to Teach or from Whom to Learn*? The teacher is to teach. He should, therefore, present a good model of teaching.
3. *Why to Teach or Why to Learn*? Education should not be taken in terms of traditional 3 R's, i.e. reading, writing and arithmetic, but in terms of 7 R's, i.e. reading, writing, arithmetic, recreation, rights, responsibilities and relationships.
4. *What to Teach or What to Learn*? This includes the acquisition of the knowledge, skills and behaviour.
5. *How to Teach*? The teacher must be well-versed with the technology of teaching.
6. *How to Learn*? The teacher and the learner must fully understand that learning takes place through mutual cooperation. A learner learns maximum when he is motivated. The teacher, therefore, has to provide motivational situations so that the learner is at his best. He has to be fully conversant with learning theories and teaching strategies.
7. *What to Teach or When to Learn*? This is concerned with creating motivational situations for the learner.

8. *Where to Teach or Where to Learn*? The school should not be taken as the only place of imparting or receiving education. It is one of the agencies of education; of course, the most important one.

KINDS/TYPES OF LEARNING: PRIME AND CONCOMITANT LEARNING

It is very difficult to classify learning into clear-cut categories because one category overlaps the other.

Chart Showing Broad Kinds of Learning

(1) Prime or Conscious Learning
(2) Concomitant or Unconscious Learning
(3) Developmental Learning
(4) General Learning
(5) Hierarchical Learning

Prime and Concomitant Learning: As a matter of fact, there are only two broad categories of learning, i.e., Prime learning and Concomitant learning.

Prime learning is deliberate, formal as well as non-formal, purposeful and systematised. It includes all types of learning except concomitant learning. All aspects of the entire instructional programme, i.e., curriculum, textbooks, methods of teaching and evaluation etc. are related to prime learning. Most of the changes in behaviour take place through prime learning.

Concomitant learning is that learning which comes in a casual manner without any direct intention to learn but on some occasions it becomes very powerful. Concomitant learning in a broad sense takes place under the indirect influence of the home, the school and the society. Students learn so many things in the school in a casual manner. It is sometimes called incidental learning. We are reminded of the learning of King Robert Bruce from the efforts of a spider. After making several unsuccessful attempts, ultimately it achieved its objective. The King, who had been unsuccessful in defeating his enemies, picked up courage like the spider again and succeeded. It was not deliberate learning.

It is said that a student gets one-fourth of his learning from his teacher (Prime learning), another fourth from his intellect (Prime learning), another fourth from his fellow students (Prime learning) and the rest (Concomitant learning) through his general experience in various situations.

MAKING LEARNING EFFECTIVE: ROLE OF THE SCHOOL AND THE TEACHERS

Learning is influenced by various conditions of life at home and school. As far as home conditions are considered, i.e., heredity and other influences of the home, very little can be done by the school to modify these. However, schools can ensure that students are given adequate opportunities to develop their hereditary endowment.

The schools should take the following steps to promote learning in the learners to their optimum levels.

1. *Healthy Physical Conditions in the School*: Unsuitable furniture in the class-room (i.e., desks and chairs and blackboards etc.), bad ventilation, over crowding etc. affect the rate of learning and the general response of the learners.

Teachers' health, voice and speech etc. also affect learning.

Therefore, all possible attempts should be made to provide healthy physical environment.

2. *Stimulation and the Role of the Teacher*: Best learning takes place when the teacher is successful in arousing the interest of the student. "The guidance of the teacher is mainly a matter of giving the right kind of stimulus to help him to learn the right things in the right way," writes Ryburn.

3. *Goals Set Before the Pupils*: A definite goal should be set before each child according to the standard expected of him. Immediate goals should be set before small children and distant goals for older ones. It must be remembered that the goals should be very clear and the children must understand these goals.

Complacency in the pupils should be avoided and in no case the pupil should feel that there is nothing more which he should learn and that there is no scope for improvement. *R. Strang* writes: "A little learning is a dangerous thing insofar as it may make a child content with what he has accomplished. The child's felt need for a skill is decreased once he has obtained enough proficiency to accomplish his immediate purpose. It is important, therefore, that as soon as the child begins to acquire skills, he should set for himself suitable specific standards of accuracy and precision."

4. *Association of Things*: Thorndike points out that things which we want to go together should be put together. Many different things should be brought together as a part of one process. Then it becomes easier to make the students understand their connection. We have discussed at various places that things can be associated in a number of ways.

5. *Guidance and Instruction*: Suitable guidance should be given to the students in selecting the best response to the environment. Demonstration is very helpful to teach various skills.

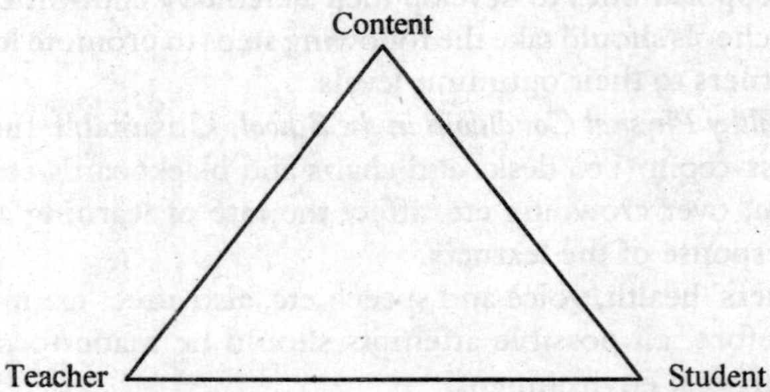

Fig. 10.2: Condition related to Content, Teacher and Student

6. *Emotional Conditions*: Children should be praised when they show good results. This gives them encouragement to show all the more better results and they develop confidence, hope, self-reliance and self-respect. Sympathetic attitude on the part of the teachers gives stimulus and a sense of security to the students. We should discard our habits of fault-finding. This develops fear and feelings of insecurity and of inferiority.

7. *Result of a Total Situation*: Learning is affected by the whole situation. It is not always possible to estimate the result of one individual factor. Learning is fruitful and permanent if the total situation is related to life.

In fact total situation includes all the factors that we have enumerated above. Learning is influenced both by heredity and environment. There is a lot that can be done by the teachers to facilitate learning.

Summing Up

Internal classroom factors which affect learning and improvement are: (1) Goals or Purposes, (2) Motivation, (3) Interest, (4) Attention, (5) Drill or Practice, (6) Boredom or Fatigue, (7) Aptitude, (8) Attitude, (9) Emotional factors—Instincts, (10) Speed, Accuracy and Retention, (11) Age, (12) Learning activities provided by the teacher, (13) Testing, (14) Guidance.

11 Motivation

MEANING OF MOTIVATION

The word motivation has been derived from the Latin word '*Motum*' which means to 'move', 'motor' and 'motion'. Motivation is an internal force which accelerates a response or behaviour. Some learners learn the same subject matter or task more efficiently than others, some find it more rewarding and interesting than others; and some enjoy it more than others. At any given time learners vary in the extent to which they are willing to direct their energies to the attainment of goals, due to difference in motivation.

The difference in their performance can be due to differences either in their abilities or in their willingness to perform as best as possible. The performance of an individual is considered as a product function of two different variables as follows:

1. A learner's ability/capacity to perform the work;
2. A learner's willingness to use his ability to perform the work.

In algebric terms, if P stands for performance in learning, C stands for capacity to learn and M stands for willingness to use capacity to learn, then P may be expressed as follows:

Thus, given the ability, it is the willingness of the learners which determines whether they will be more efficient or less. Similarly, given the willingness, it is the ability of learners which determines whether they will be more efficient or less.

Performance = Capacity to learn × Willingness to use capacity to learn
$P = C \times M$

Thus, given the ability, it is the willingness of the learners which determines whether they will be more efficient or less. Similarly, given the willingness, it is the ability of learners which determines whether they will be more efficient or less.

How to make learners performance more or better is an issue that requires an understanding of what motivates learners to do so.

The following definitions throw adequate light on the meaning of motivation:

1. *Arun Monappa and Mirza S. Saiyadain*: "Motivation is propensity or the level of desire of an individual to behave in a certain manner at a certain time and in a certain situation."
2. *C.W. Goods*: "Motivation is the process of sustaining and regulating activity."
3. *D.O. Hebb*: "The term motivation refers (i) to existence of an organised phase sequence, (ii) to its direction and content, (iii) to its persistence in given direction or stability of content."
4. *F.G. McDonald*: "Motivation is an energy change within the person characterised by affective arousal and anticipatory goal relations."
5. *T.W. Atkinson*: "The term motivation refers to the arousal of tendency to act to produce one or more effects."

Sources of Motivation

Motivation has the following four sources:
1. Needs, 2. Drives, 3. Incentives, 4. Motives.

Motives: Psychologists do not agree on the meaning of the term 'motives'. These have been defined as follows:

1. *E.C. Murray*: Motive is an internal factor that arouses, directs and integrates a person's behaviour.
2. *Alice Crow*: Motives can be regarded as those internal conditions or forces that tend to impel an individual towards certain goals.
3. *Shoffer and Others*: Motive is a tendency to an activity initiated by a drive and concluded by the adjustment.
4. *M.C. Dougall*: Motive is a condition, physiological and psychological, within the individual that disposes it to act in certain ways.

5. *All Port*: A motive is any internal condition in the person that induces action or thought.
6. *Arun Monappa and Mirza S. Saiyadain*: Motivation is propensity or the level of desire of an individual to behave in a certain manner at a certain time and in a certain situation.
7. *Bernard*: Motivation is the stimulation of actions towards a particular objective where previously there was little or no attraction to that goal.
8. *Goods*: Motivation is the process of arousing, sustaining and regulating activity.
9. *Harold Koontz and Cyril O'Donnell*: Motivation refers to the drive and effort to satisfy a want or goal.
10. *Guilford*: A motive is any particular internal factor or condition that tends to initiate and sustain activity.
11. *Lovell*: Motivation is defined more formally as psycho-physiological or internal process initiated by some need which leads to activity which will satisfy that need.
12. *Skinner*: Motivation in school learning involves arousing, persisting, sustaining and directing desirable behaviour.
13. *Gates*: Motives are conditions—Psychological and physiological with the organism that dispose it to act in a certain way.
14. *Blair*: Arising from our needs motives are the energies which give direction and purpose in behaviour.

Motives are expressions of a person's needs and hence they are personal and internal. Need here means something within an individual that prompts him to action. Motives or needs are 'whys' of behaviour. Motives are the primary energisers of behaviour which prompt people to action. Motives give direction to human behaviour because they are directed towards achievement of certain 'goals'.

Types of Motives

We can divide motives in various ways:

A. *Primary Motives and Secondary Motives*

Primary Motives are the biological or physiological motives. The examples of such motives are: hunger, thirst, sex, sleep, rest, etc.

These motives ensure the preservation of life for the individual and for his race. An important feature of these motives is that they are inborn and *innate*.

Secondary Motives are psychological and social motives. Examples of such motives are: need for security, achievement, gaining status and recognition, etc. These motives are acquired like other forms of learning behaviour, when we are trying to satisfy our needs.

B. *Innate and Acquired Motives*

Innate motives are known as physiological motives and are associated with the birth of the individual. Examples are: hunger, thirst, sleep, sex, etc.

Acquired motives are learnt motives. Examples are: habit, interest, etc.

C. *Natural and Artificial Motives*

Natural motives are present in the individual by birth. Examples are play, prestige, etc.

Artificial motives are complementary motives to natural motives. Examples are: reward, punishment, etc.

Thus motivation refers to the process by which human needs direct and control the behaviour of a human being. Motivation may also be defined as the process which inspires the people at work to contribute to the best of their capability for the achievement of organisational objectives. In other words, motivation may be defined as the process of stimulating people to action to accomplish desired goals. In simple terms, creation of a will to work or to work more or better is motivation.

Nature and Characteristics of Motivation

The characteristics of motives highlight the nature of motivation.

1. *Personal and Internal*: Motives are personal, internal and invisible because, these are expressions of a person's needs. Motives are the energising forces within us. Motivation is a psychological phenomenon which arises from the feeling of needs and wants of learners.

2. *Different from Learner to Learner*: Motives differ from learner to learner because every learner has his own set of needs at a particular point of time.
3. *Different from Time to Time*: Motives energising us differ from time to time. Motives come and go. A motive need not have the same energy potential at all points of time.
4. *Different Behaviour from Same Motive*: One motive may result in many different behaviours.
5. *Same Behaviour from Different Motives*: The same behaviour may result from different motives. That is why a motive cannot be identified from any specific behaviour.
6. *Continuous Process*: Motivation is a continuous process because human needs are unlimited and fulfilment of one set of needs gives rise to another set of needs.
7. *Pervasive Function*: Motivation is required in all types of organisations (commercial, educational, social, religious, political, small or large) and at all levels. However, its ways, methods, forms and types may differ at different levels.
8. *Behaviour for Estimating Motives*: Repeated behaviour can be used as an estimate of learner motives. It is possible to get repeated observations of one learner's behaviour and then make an estimate of the cause of that behaviour.
9. *Operate in Harmony or in Conflict*: Motives can operate in harmony or in conflict. For example, a learner may want to get high marks in school while also wanting to help his father in the business.
10. *Interact with the Environment*: Motives interact with the environment.
11. *Causes Goal-Directed Behaviour*: Motives cause goal directed behaviour.

PROCESS AND IMPORTANCE OF MOTIVATION

Process of Motivation

The elements of the process of motivation are:

(1) Motives, (2) Behaviour, (3) Goal, (4) Feedback. The process of motivation has been shown below:

1. *Motive*: Motives prompt learners to action. Motives determine the general direction of learner's behaviour.
2. *Behaviour*: Behaviour is a series of activities of an individual. It is generally motivated by a desire to achieve a goal.
3. *Goal*: Motives are directed towards goals. Goals are the ends which provide satisfaction of human wants.
4. *Feedback*: Feedback may be in the form of reduction or increase in tension.

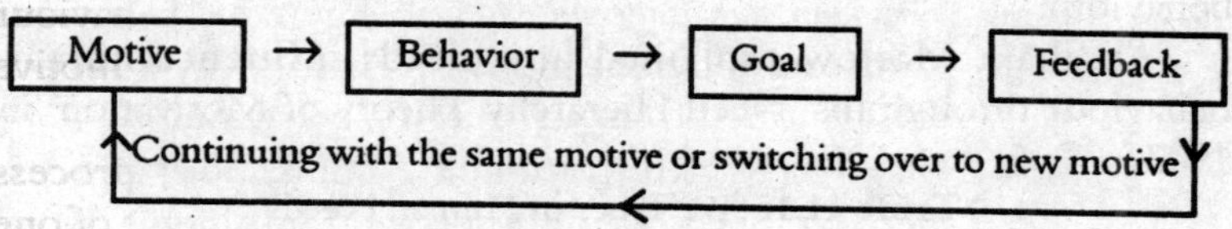

Importance of Motivation

Motivation is the core of learning. The importance of motivation arises from the benefits which flow from it. These benefits are shown below:

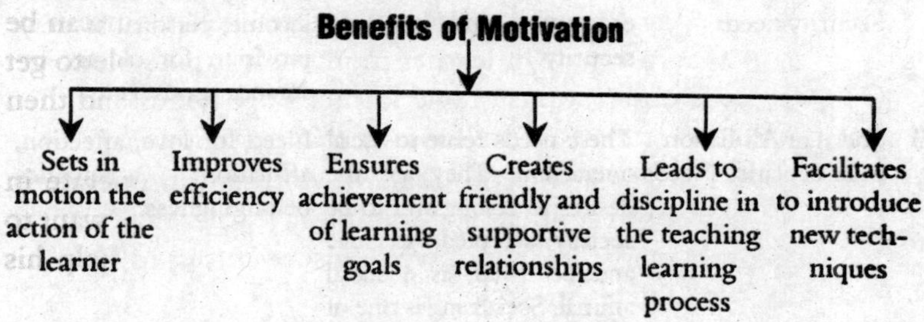

Fig. 11.1: Importance of Motivation

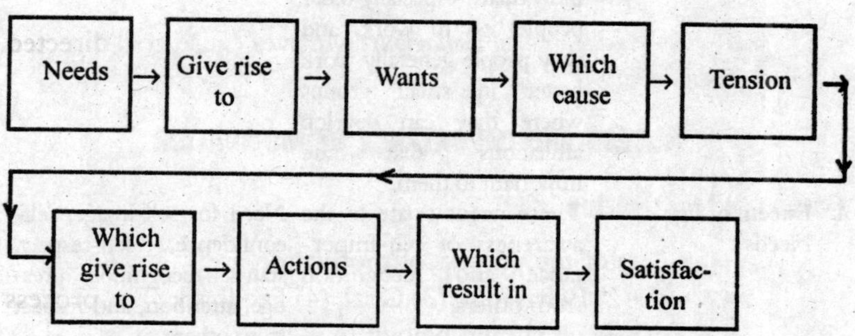

Fig. 11.2: Motivational Cycle: Needs—Satisfaction Chain

MASLOW'S NEED—THEORY OF MOTIVATION

To get work done with the cooperation of learners for the attainment of learning objectives every teacher must study the behaviour of learner. To determine their needs and provide an environment in which appropriate incentives are available for their need satisfaction. Human needs serve as driving force in human behaviour.

Abraham Maslow explained how needs influence human behaviour through his 'Need Hierarchy Theory of Motivation' in 1943.

Table 11.1: Five Types of Human Needs

Need	*Meaning*	*Examples*
1. Physiological needs	These needs relate to the survival and maintenance of human life.	Need for food, clothing, shelter, air, water.
2. Safety needs or Security needs	These needs relate to the economic and physical security.	Security of source of income, personal security, provision for old-age insurance against risks.
3. Social or Affiliation or Acceptance Needs	These needs relate to social interaction. They are the desires to belong and to be socially accepted, to love and be loved, as a social animal. Socialising is one of those reasons why many individuals (especially older people) go to work, and why people generally work better in small groups where they can develop affiliations that are important to them.	Need for love, affection, affiliation, acceptance belongingness.
4. Esteem or Ego Needs	These needs relate to the awareness of self-importance and recognition from others.	Need for self-image, self-confidence, self-respect, status, recognition prestige, attention, and respect from others.

(*Contd.*)

Need	*Meaning*	*Examples*
5. Self-Actualisation or Self-fulfillment needs	These needs relate to self-fulfillment, are the desires to realize one's own full creative potential through creativity, self-expression and self-development to become what one is capable of becoming.	Need to grow, sense of fulfillment, maximum self-development, personal achievement.

Hierarchy of Human Needs

Maslow proposed that human needs can be arranged in a particular order (i.e., hierarchy) of their importance or prepotency) from the lower to the higher level needs. Physiological needs are placed at the lowest level of hierarchy of needs. Then safety needs, social needs and esteem needs are positioned in ascending order. Self-actualisation needs are placed at the highest level of hierarchy of needs. (Fig. 11.3)

Merits of Maslow's Need Hierarchy

Following are the merits of Maslow's Need Hierarchy:

1. It is simple to understand and has an intuitive appeal.
2. It recognises the spectrum of human needs and indicates how humans are motivated in their work behaviour.
3. Its basic proposition that deprivation of a need dominates behaviours, seems to be quite sound.
4. It provides some guidance to teachers and educational administrators.
   (a) Identification of unfulfilled needs among the various learners.
   (b) Designing of measures to satisfy unsatisfied needs as a means of motivation.
   (c) Designing of measures to arouse new higher level needs.

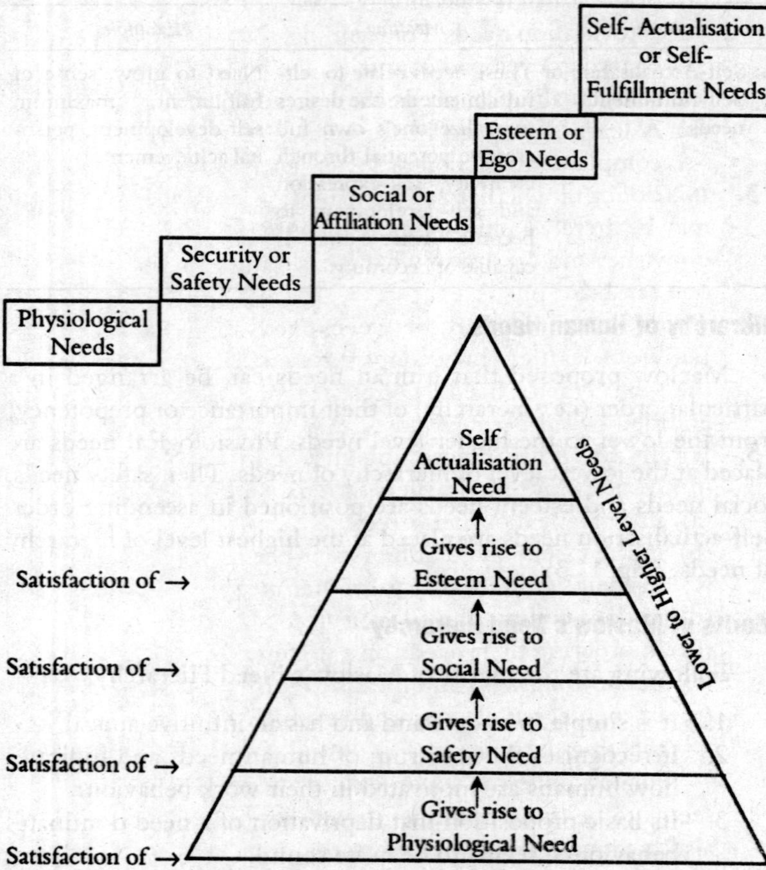

Fig. 11.3: Maslow's Hierarchy of Needs

Criticisms of Maslow's Theory

Maslow's theory is subject to the following criticisms:

1. It is not amenable for empirical validation on account of complexity of developing meaningful measures for various needs.
2. The hierarchy appears to be rigid. The learners need not necessarily follow a step-by-step way of meeting their needs for example—

(a) Some learners may not be aware of esteem and self-actualisation needs. For example, for majority learning of underdeveloped countries, higher level esteem and self-actualisation needs have no meaning.

(b) A learner may go in for higher level needs before complete satisfaction of lower level needs.

3. It is doubtful whether Self-actualisation is a need or not. It may be merely a philosophical and ethical aspiration based on wishes and dreams of what one should be than on what one can be or one is.
4. There is a direct link between needs and motivation. Different learners may adopt different practices to fulfil the same type of needs. Different types of needs may be gratified by similar methods.
5. It fails to clarify the complexity of human needs and motivation since the learners differ:

(a) in awareness of their needs;
(b) in the extent and depth of their needs;
(c) in their willingness to fulfil their needs;
(d) in their ability to fulfil their needs;
(e) in ordering their needs on a preference scale;
(f) in choosing ways and means to fulfil their needs;
(g) in the degree of gratification which they desire from meeting their needs.

For example, for some learners need for self-esteem seems to be more prominent than that of love. There are also creative learners in whom the drive for creativeness seems to be more important. In certain learners the level of motivation may be permanently lower.

6. Need may not necessarily be the only factor which influences a learner's behaviour at a particular point of time. There may be other factors which may affect the behaviour at that time.
7. It is also doubtful—

(i) Whether deprivation of a need dominates behaviour at all. It may not motivate the learner in a unidirectional positive manner. It may even lead to his depression, diversion, frustration and inaction.

(ii) Whether relative gratification of needs at a particular level drives the learners to move to next higher level needs.

(iii) Whether a satisfied need motivates a learner. He may remain at that level and continue to seek need fulfilment in a routine manner. Several needs recur in cycles, short or long, and hence satisfaction could not be a permanent or one time affair.

(iv) One need is satisfied at one time. The phenomenon of multiple motivation is of great practical importance in understanding the behaviour of the learner. A learner's behaviour at any time is mostly guided by multiplicity of motives.

Intrinsic and Extrinsic Motivation

Intrinsic Motivation: It comes into display when the resolution of tension is to be found in mastering the learning task itself. The material learned provides its own reward. For example, the student who studies the construction of model dams diligently so that he can make a model, is experiencing a king of intrinsic motivation.

Extrinsic Motivation: It occurs when a student pursues a learning task for reasons which are external. If a student engages in construction of model dams because he thinks it will please his father, who is an ex-engineer, this becomes a case of extrinsic motivation. Motivation is probably a function of an interactive situation where reward for a particular action acts as an incentive. Some of the common forms of extrinsic motivation are:

(a) Purposive goals
(b) Knowledge of results
(c) Punishments and rewards
(d) Praise and blame
(e) Rivalry

TECHNIQUES OF ENHANCING LEARNER'S MOTIVATION

The teaching-learning process aims at maximum learning in a minimum period of time. It is, therefore, necessary that children should be properly motivated and the teacher should be conversant with important ways of motivating children.

1. *Child-Centred Approach*: The child is the focal point in the learning process. The teachers, therefore, should keep in view the needs, interests and aptitudes of children while planning for their education.
2. *Law of Association*: The child is easily motivated to learn new knowledge if he thinks that he knows all that is required as a base for new learning. This enables him to master new facts and acquire knowledge.
3. *Progressive Methods of Teaching*: The teacher should use new methods like the Montessori Methods, the K.G. Method, the Project Method and the Dalton Plan as methods of teaching. These methods are child-centred and based on important psychological principles.
4. *Use of Teaching-Learning Aids*: The teacher should introduce various aids and devices of teaching, for example, audio-visual aids, radio, television, etc. to create interest in learning. These will motivate children in grasping and digesting new learning.
5. *Element of Success*: The teacher should divide new learning into smaller and smaller tasks and assign them to the different students of the class. Children will complete them in a short period of time and will have a feeling of success. It is this feeling of success, which will motivate them for future achievement and success.
6. *Learning by Doing*: Children are active by nature. They want to do something with their hands. Let this need of the children be satisfied. A satisfied child is always a well-motivated child.
7. *Sense of Achievement in the Child*: The teacher should keep an eye on the progress of every child. He should maintain a proper record of the same. He should inform his pupils about the success achieved by them, after two or three months. This will develop a sense of achievement among the pupils. This will also lead to achievement – motivation.
8. *Group Work*: Children like group life. They may be divided into various groups. Group work leads to quicker, better and easier learning.

9. *Value of Learning*: The teacher should highlight the value of learning among his pupils. They should realise that 'knowledge is power' and can be helpful in life and will make them successful.
10. *Ego-Involvement*: The personality of the child should be given its due recognition.
11. *Healthy Environment*: A healthy class-room environment in itself is a great motivating force.
12. *Constructive and Creative Discipline*: The teacher's attitude towards his children should be sympathetic but firm.
13. *Stimulus Variation and the Teacher*: It has been generally observed that children are not able to attend to one thing for a very long period. The effectiveness of the teaching-learning process in such a situation depends to a great extent on the stimulus variations used by the teacher behaviour. Some of the common teacher behaviours in the class-room which fall under variation are:
    (a) Teacher movement
    (b) Teacher gestures
    (c) Changes in speech pattern
    (d) Changes in sensory focus
    (e) Changes in postures
14. *Reinforcement: Praise and Blame*: These may be classified as:
    (a) *Positive Verbal Reinforcement*: Following a pupil's answer, the teacher verbally indicates pleasures at the pupil's response by the use of words like 'Good', 'Fair', 'Excellent', 'Correct', etc.
    (b) *Positive Non-Verbal Reinforcement*: These include:
    Nods and smiles.
    Teacher's friendly movements towards pupils.
    Teacher's friendly look.

12

Memory and Forgetting

SIGNIFICANCE OF MEMORY

There is no doubt that memory is one of the best friends, guides and philosophers of an individual. Memory enables a person to be efficient, both individually and socially. Memory enables us to remember and recall important facts, ideas, names etc. One of the important functions of school instruction is, therefore, to encourage the students develop good and sharp memory to use in school life for the purpose of examination and evaluation etc. and also to meet out-of-school life problems successfully.

MEANING OF MEMORY

Memory may be defined as the function of the mind by virtue of which it records, retains and processes ideas.

According to Woodworth, four main elements of memory are: learning (acquisition), retention, recall and recognition.

Learning: It is the process of establishing association of the ideas in mind.

Retention: It is the process of relegation of the past experience in the sub-conscious mind of the individual in the form of a mental experience.

Recall: It is bringing again to mind the past experience on the basis of association of ideas.

Recall is of two types: (1) Spontaneous and (2) Deliberate. In spontaneous recall we make no effort to recall but the experience or ideas just flow. In deliberate recall, we make an effort to recall something.

Recall is dependent on association of ideas. This association of ideas is dependent on these laws: (i) Law of Similarity, (ii) Law of Contrast, (iii) Law of Contiguity, (iv) Law of Regency, (v) Law of Frequency, (vi) Law of Primacy, and (vii) Law of Vividness.

Recognition: It is the capacity to recognise or express knowledge of all—seeing a thing that has been seen earlier.

DEFINITIONS OF MEMORY

Some of the important definitions of memory are given below. These illustrate the various elements involved in memory.

1. James Drever in *Dictionary of Psychology* has defined memory as "The characteristic of living organisms in virtue of what they experience leaves behind effects which modify future experience and behaviour."
2. Woodworth and Marquis say, "Memory consists in recalling what has been previously learnt."
3. Stout defines memory as the "ideal revival", i.e. to revive the things, objects or experiences in the same order and form.
4. Ross defines memory as "a new experience determined by the disposition laid down by previous experiences and the relation between the two being clearly apprehended."
5. J.A. Adams—Memory is the "learning capacity for responding, and its persistence over time is measured by the retention test. Memory is the state of a subject that gives the capability for correct occurrence of a criterion response. There is an initial acquisition session in which the subject makes a discriminative response to a stimulus, followed by a period of time called the retentional interval when the criterion response does not occur."

MEMORY SYSTEM

Information from the environment arrives through the senses and is held briefly in a sensory store (the sensory register) of relatively large capacity. Some of this incoming information, once it is identified and categorised, can be passed along to the short-term store and then to the long-term store.

Short-term Store: It is assumed to be a temporary working memory with a quite limited capacity. In a sense, this is a record of the current contents of consciousness.

Long-term Store: It is conceived of as a permanent repository of information. This memory store contains essentially, our knowledge of the world, and its capacity is assumed to be very great. Once material has been transferred to long-term store, there seems to be very little—if any loss of information.

As material is acquired, it presumably passes through the sensory register and into the short-term store. Control process such as rehearsal permits the transfer of this material to long-term store, from which it may be subsequently retrieved. Actually, although not indicated in this diagram, long-term store enters the picture in a number of different ways. First, information from long-term store is necessary to permit pattern recognition and identification of raw sensory information held in the sensory register. Second, information that has been sufficiently rehearsed or organised is thought to be transferred to long-term store. Finally, the very control processes that are assumed to govern the movement of the information through the system must be represented in some way (as rules) in long-term store (see Fig. 12.1).

Immediate and Permanent Memory: The span of immediate memory is very wide. An example of immediate memory is memory near the examination. When things or ideas etc. are recalled after sometime, it is called long-term memory or permanent memory. Immediate memory is also called Short Term Memory (STM) and Permanent Memory as Long Term Memory (LTM).

(ii) *Personal and Impersonal Memory*: When personal experiences are recalled, it is called personal memory and when dry facts are recalled, it is called impersonal memory.

(iii) *Active and Passive Memory*: When effort is made to remember things, it is active memory and when things come to mind automatically, it is passive memory.

(iv) *Rote Memory/Logical Memory*: In rote memory, there is no understanding of things, and when things are learnt by insight, it is logical memory.

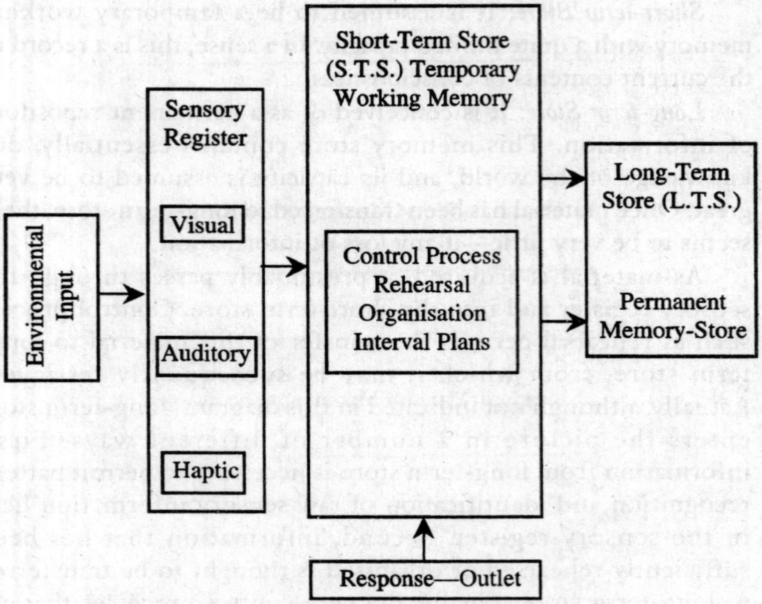

Movement of Information within Memory System

Fig. 12.1: An Overview of Memory System

KINDS AND TYPES OF MEMORY

Kinds and Types of Memory: Classification I

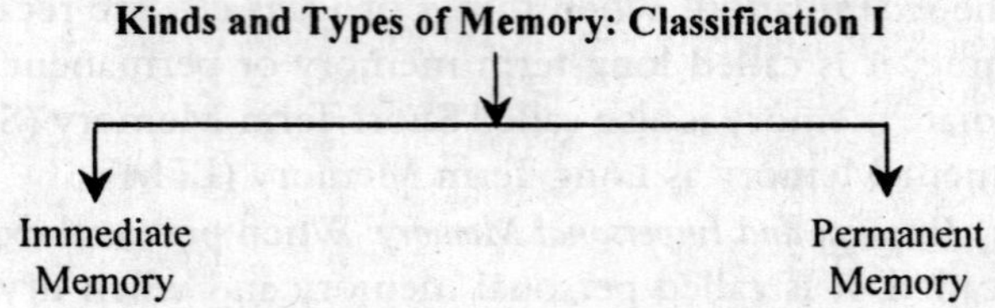

Kinds and Types of Memory: Classification II

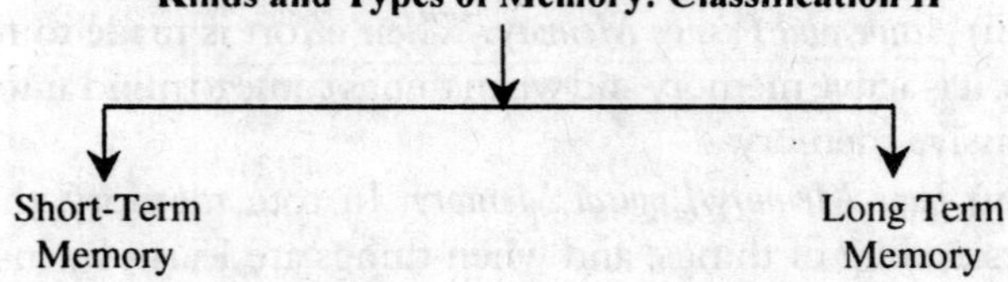

Kinds andTypes of Memory: Classification III

- Personal Memory
- Impersonal Memory

Kinds and Types of Memory: Classification IV

- Active Memory
- Positive Memory

Kinds and Types of Memory: Classification V

- Rote Memory
- Logical Memory

FACTORS CONTRIBUTING TO GOOD MEMORY

Factors Contributing to Good Memory: Classification I

- (1) Factors Relating to the Learner
- (2) Factors Relating to Different Types of Material
- (3) Factors Relating to Retention or Retention as Affected by Original learning

General Factors Contributing to Good Memory: Classification II

- (1) Health of the Learner
- (2) Attentiveness of the Learner
- (3) Distinct and Vivid Impressions
- (4) Repetition Insight

1. Factors in the Learner:

These are as under:

(i) Age of the learner.
(ii) Intelligence of the learner.
(iii) Mental state of the learner.
(iv) Physical state of the learner.
(v) Health of the learner.
(vi) Attitude of the learner.

2. Factors Relating to the Subject Matter or Types of Materials to be Learnt

(i) Meaningful of the material.
(ii) Pleasantness of the material.

3. Factors in Retention or Retention as Affected by Original Learning

(a) *Will to Remember*: The mental set with which the material is learnt enhances retention. When one is motivated to learn, this leads to better attention and better retention.

(b) *Recitation increases* the amount retained.

(c) Materials learnt by *distributed practice* are better retained than those learnt by massed practice.

(d) *Associations Also Help Retain Better*: Most of us remember while learning arithmetic problems of simple fraction. We associate the technique with the word 'BODMAS' and this leads to better retention of the procedure of simplification.

(e) Material learnt by the *whole method* is better retained than that learnt by the part method. But relative efficiency of the whole method also depends upon the nature of the material learnt.

(f) *Over-learnt* material is better retained. Over-learning is the term applied to learning beyond the stage where the material can be said to have been learnt.

SIGNS OF GOOD MEMORY

Psychologists identify five signs of good memory.

1. *Rapidity*: The first sign of good memory is rapidity, i.e., how

quickly the learner recalls his experiences. How little time the learner takes in recalling his experience is denoted by rapidity.

2. *Accuracy*: This implies the exactness with which a past experience is recalled. There may be rapidity in memory but accuracy may be missing. A good memory must possess these elements simultaneously.
3. *Length of Time*: This element denotes the time for which one can retain the past experiences and recalls them accurately. One individual may be able to retain and recall only a small quantity of the experience while another is able to retain and recall a large quantity of the experience. The latter has relatively a good memory.
4. *Quantity of Experience*: Some persons are able to recall whatever they learn while others can recall only a little.
5. *Promptness*: It implies the ease and spontaneity with which experience is recalled.
6. *Serviceableness*: It refers to the recall of right experience at the right time at the right place and in the right manner.

METHODS OF MEASUREMENT OF RETENTION

Recall Method or Reproduction Method

For instance, the learner may learn a list of 40 words and after 8 hours he is able to recall or reproduce only 20 words. Thus his recall store is 20 out of 40 words or 50 per cent.

Methods of Measurement of Retention

(1) Recall or Reproduction Method
(2) Relearning Method
(3) Recognition Method
(4) Reconstruction Method

Relearning or Saving Method: In this method we first calculate the number of trials taken to learn the material in the beginning and then note down the saving of trials on relearning it after some lapse of time. For example, if the subject takes 10 trials to recite a whole poem correctly, and only takes 6 trials to master the same after 2 days, his saving score would be:

$$\frac{10-6}{10}=\frac{4}{10} \text{ or } 40\%$$

Recognition Method: In a typical recognition test, the learner's ability to recognise items he has just studied is tested by showing him the study items together with new items and asking the learner to identify the study items.

Method of Reconstruction: In this method, the learner first learns material in a serial order and then the items of the learning material are mixed up and shuffled. Then the learner is required to rearrange the items in their proper sequence.

GENERAL CHARACTERISTICS OF CHILDREN'S MEMORY AND ADULT'S MEMORY

Children's Memory	*Adult's Memory*
1. Children commit to memory without any logic.	1. Adults have a logical memory. They observe facts intelligently and organise them logically in their mental make up. This makes assimilation of facts possible.
2. Children have a mechanical memory. It is by mechanical repetition that they remember facts.	2. Adults have an understanding memory.
3. Children learn more quickly and retain their impressions in a better way about concrete things.	3. Adults have better memory of concrete things as well as abstract ideas.
4. Memory of children is short-lived. They are not able to retain it for long.	4. Adults have relatively a long-lived memory.
5. Children's memory is passive.	5. Adults have an active memory.
6. Children recall facts spontaneously. Past experiences are recalled without any effort.	6. They have to make a conscious and deliberate effort to recall facts.

ECONOMICAL METHODS OF MEMORISING

Following are the important economical methods of memorising.

1. *Principle of Association*: The law of association is very helpful in memorisation.
2. *Law of Exercise and Intelligent Repetition*: Repetition and its quality affects memorising. Several psychological experiments have shown that the items repeated more often are remembered longer than those repeated less. However, repetition should be with understanding.
3. *Spaced Repetition*: The material to be committed to memory should be repeated at intervals with periods of rest. This will save the learner from fatigue. Effort-rest-Effort will lead to better memorisation.
4. *Use of Progressive Methods of Teaching-Learning*: The project method and the problem method are very helpful in making the matter interesting. Students assimilate easily and retain for a longer period.
5. *Use of Modern Technology*: A variety of aids should be used in the teaching-learning process to make the students motivated in the lesson. They help in enhancing the concentration of the students.
6. *Whole or Part Method*: There are two methods of memorising any content of learning which are known as the *Whole method* and the *Part method*. We may give an example of a poem which the child wants to memorise.

According to the *whole method* the child may read the whole poem again and again from the beginning to the end and thus memorise it.

According to the *part method*, the poem may be divided into smaller units and the child may try to memorise each part intelligently until the skill related to that learning has been fully acquired.

THE WHOLE METHOD AND PART METHOD

The Whole Method: Advantages

1. The parts are combined into one and give a meaning to the child.

2. If the child has learnt some content material by heart, this method works.

Limitations: This method does not operate if the subject matter for memorisation is too long and difficult.

The Part Method

Advantages

1. It works well when the subject matter of learning is short.
2. It gives better results if the learner is young and the subject matter is difficult.

Limitations

1. The structure of the entire poem is not clear to the child till the end of the learning.
2. The child finds it difficult to link the parts of the poem into the whole poem.
3. It is psychologically unsound.

Latest Researches

1. Aveling came to the conclusion that nearly one-fifth of the time of learning can be economised with the wise use of the whole method.
2. Pyne and Syner came to the conclusion that the whole method is more effective when the poem has about 240 lines.

The Part Progressive Method or Mediating Method

A modification of the Whole method is suggested which is known as Part Progressive or Mediating Method. The outlines are as follows:

1. The difficult words or phrases may be mastered or understood before hand and then the whole method may be employed.
2. The learner should make a cautious approach while making use of the whole method.
3. The poem may be sub-divided into three units. The child

may combine 1 and 2 and later on combine 2 and 3 and finally 1, 2 and 3.

The Recitation Method

Features

1. In this method, the learner first reads the matter once or twice and then recites and recalls that matter without looking at the matter.
2. The learner evaluates himself from time to time and notes down those points which he has not been able to recall.
3. Small children really recite their lessons in a sing-song manner with a rhythm.

Advantages of the Method

1. The learner is able to constantly evaluate himself and find out his limitations.
2. This leads to concentrated attention as the weak links in his learning are strengthened.
3. The child is able to find out his own mistakes and thus explores new avenues of further improvement.
4. The learner comes to have a sense of achievement leading to further effort.
5. It saves the efforts of the teacher in the learning process.
6. In case of small children the rhyme and rhythm help to fix up words in the mind and enable the child to enjoy the music. This enjoyment leads to retention and memorisation.
7. The subject matter is learnt as it to be used. Little transfer is necessary in the later reproduction.

Spaced and Unspaced Methods of Learning

Spaced or Distributed Method of Learning: In this type of learning the child is not required to memorise the entire subject-matter in one continuous sitting. After learning for some time some rest is given to the child. The principle of 'work and rest' is followed.

If the child has to memorise a poem, he at the initial stage is advised to go on repeating it for many times. After repetition, he takes rest for some time. After rest the child again repeats the poem and takes rest. In this way with repeated intervals of work and rest he will be able to have mastery over the poem or any other assigned work.

Unspaced or Spaced Method: The child has to memorise the assigned work in one sitting without any interval or rest. The learning goes on continuously without any interruption till it is mastered.

Suggestions: Many experimental studies have been conducted to assess the relative values of these two methods. It has been found that:

1. In-short lessons unspaced method of leaning may be followed.
2. In giving lessons spaced method of learning should be followed. One suggested modification is that it is better to distribute the hours of work in the sittings of the child and also introduce the periods of rest in between these sittings. This helps in removing the monotony caused by long periods of study. Rest keeps away the fatigue element and the attention also does not flag. The child feels fresh after a period of rest and his interest is kept alive.

Improvement of Development of Memory: Suggestions

Memory may be improved by following the techniques as give below:

1. *Law of Exercise and Intelligent Repetition*: Repetition and its quality affects memorising. Several psychological experiments have shown that the items repeated more often are remembered longer than those repeated less. However, repetition should be with understanding.
2. *Spaced Repetition*: The material to be committed to memory should be repeated at intervals with periods of rest. This will save the learner from fatigue. Effort-rest-effort-will lead to better memorisation.

3. *Use of Modern Technology*: A variety of aids should be used in the teaching-learning process to make the students motivated in the lesson. They help in enhancing the concentration of the students.
4. *Use of Progressive Methods of Teaching-Learning*: The project method and the problem method are very helpful in making the matter interesting. Students assimilate easily and retain for a longer period.
5. *Interest*: For proper memorising, interest in the topic or subject is essential. There is a popular saying 'you can take the horse to water for drinking but you cannot make him drink unless he is interested in drinking'. Similar is the case with the children.
6. *Motivation in Learning*: Motivation creates interest and produces the right condition for memorisation.
7. *Will*: Will to learn a topic or subject enhances interest and motivation and thereby it leads to better retention.
8. *Association*: The law of association is very helpful in memorisation.
9. *Over-learning*: Over-learning implies practice that continues after a perfect recall has been established. Over-learning leads to better retention. However, over-learning should be moderate. Expensive over-learning will lead to boredom. Under-learning hinders retention.
10. *Use of Mnemonics*: Mnemonics devices are useful in retaining several types of material. Through this device, information in the brain is deliberately transformed into meaningful system to improve memory. For instance, aims of education may be memorised with the aid of 7 R's. 7 R's denote Reading, Writing, Arithmetic, Rights, Responsibilities and Recreation.

    Three A's may represent Age, Ability and Aptitude of students while referring to individual differences.

    Four H's may denote four aims of education: Development of Head, Hand, Heart and Health.
11. *Meaningful Organisation of the Subject Matter*: One of the most effective methods to improve memory or retention which teachers can use is the meaningful organisation of the

subject-matter. Approach should be logical-cum-psychological.

12. *Formation of Clear Concept*: Efforts should be made to improve memory with the help of illustrations, and various types of audio-visual aids.
13. *Principle of Learning by Doing*: Learning experiences acquired through doing are remembered for a longer period.
14. *Overall Classroom Environment*: It includes proper physical conditions and the attitude of the teacher.

Conclusion

1. It is difficult to specify which method is the best one. It may be pointed out that a single method cannot work on all occasions.
2. The abilities of the child also determine the success of the method.
3. The quantum of work also determines the methods to be adopted.
4. Environment also plays an important role in learning.
5. The will of the child determines the efficiency and effectiveness of learning.

Latest Research: Gates conducted an experiment with sixteen non-sense syllables and live short biographical materials accounting for about 170 words. He used two methods: (a) Reading and re-reading of the subject-matter by one group of students. (b) Another group was asked to follow the recitation method. Gates came to the conclusion that recitation method proved to be better than the reading and re-reading method.

Suggestion: It may be pointed out that the child should devote three-fifths of the period of study to recitation. This method will help both in the immediate and delayed recall.

FORGETTING

Meaning of Forgetting

Following are a few definition of forgetting which throw light on the concept of forgetting.

Adams—"True learning is judicious forgetting".

James Drever—"Forgetting means failure at any time to recall an experience when attempting to do so, or to perform an action previously learned".

Num—"Forgetting is failing to retain or able to recall what has been acquired".

Munn—"Forgetting is the loss permanent or temporary of the ability to recall or recognise something learned earlier".

NATURE AND CHARACTERISTICS OF FORGETTING

1. Forgetting is a process of fading with the passage of time.
2. Forgetting occurs when memories of the same type interfere with each other.
3. Forgetting is attributed to change in traces in the brain.
4. Forgetting is not losing something but rather is more like being unable to find it.
5. Forgetting is influenced by motivation.
6. Forgetting is caused by lack of proper organisation and systematisation of the learned material.
7. Forgetting takes place on account of change of stimulating conditions.

Summing up: Forgetting's nature requires more than one explanation.

CURVES OF FORGETTING

Following two curves based on Ebbinghaus illustrate the amount of forgetting with time to lapse. (Nonsense syllabus—meaningless words like Nof, bdf and cem etc.)

Table 12.1: Time Lapsed and Percentage of Amount Forgotten

Time Lapsed	*Percentage of Amount Forgotten*
20 minutes	47%
One day	66%
Two days	72%
Six days	75%
Thirtyone days	79%

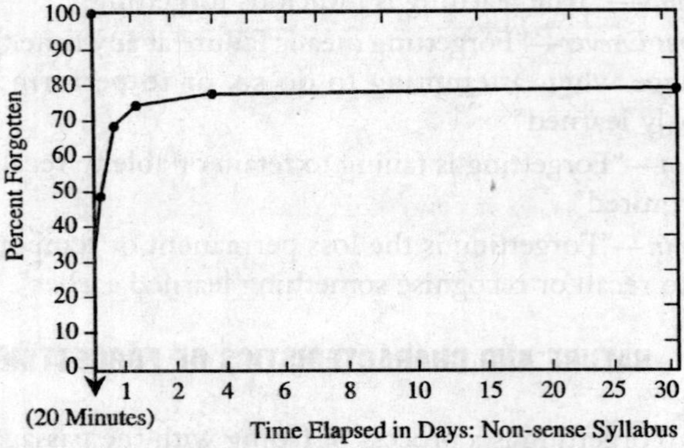

Fig. 12.2: Time Elapsed in Forgetting

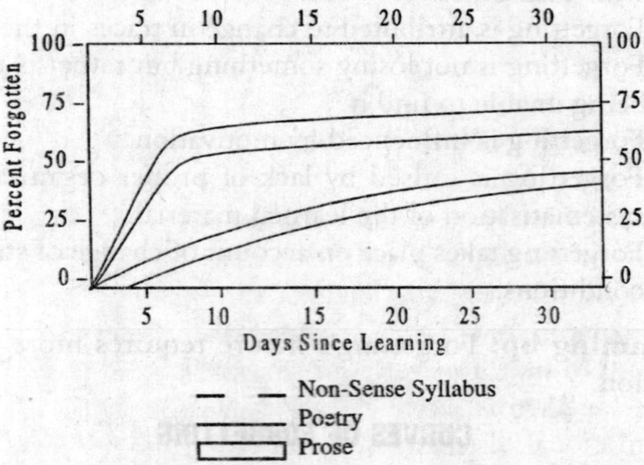

Fig. 12.3: Different Types of Forgetting

TYPES OF FORGETTING

Types of Forgetting: Classification I

- Natural Forgetting or Passive Forgetting
- Unnatural or Morbid Forgetting or Active Forgetting

Types of Forgetting: Classification II

- General Forgetting
- Specific Forgetting

Types of Forgetting: Classification III

- Physical or Organic Forgetting
- Psychological Forgetting

CAUSES AND MINIMISING FORGETFULNESS

Causes of Forgetting

1. Lack of interest in work.
2. Disuse of activity.
3. Lapse of time.
4. Lack of integration and synthesis. This may be due to:
   (i) Interference of another activity.
   (ii) Continued experience of various kinds, all serious in nature.
   (iii) No time for rest after serious activity for integration and synthesis.
5. Emotional disturbance.
6. Fatigue.
7. Morbid forgetfulness on account of unpleasant and painful experiences.

Minimising Forgetfulness

1. *Vividness*: Vivid impressions backed by illustrations and aids are better retained.
2. *Organisation of the Learning Material*: Material which is properly related and organised is easily retained than the material which is unrelated and disconnected.

3. *Recapitulation and Review*: The lesson or experience needs to be recapitulated or reviewed.
4. *Nature of Learning Material*: Meaningful material is better retained than material which is confusing.
5. *Distributed Learning*: Retention is definitely better if the learning material is spread over suitable sittings.
6. *Over-learning*: Studies have shown that an over-learned lesson is better retained than one barely learned. Of course, extreme is always bad.

13

Intelligence

MEANING OF INTELLIGENCE

Intelligence has been viewed differently by scholars. More than one hundred definitions of intelligence are found in the psychological literature. However, in general, intelligence is considered as the global capacity of an individual to think rationally, to act purposefully and to deal effectively with the environment. All the discoveries and inventions of the world are usually attributed to persons of high intelligence.

Here some of the most prominent definition of intelligence are given. These definition throw meaningful light on the meaning, nature and development of intelligence.

1. *Binet* describes intelligence as: (1) the tendency of thought to take and maintain a definite direction, (2) the capacity to make adaptations for the purpose of attaining a desired end, and (3) the power of self-criticism.
2. *Colvin* defines it as capacity to learn.
3. *Burt* calls it the power of readjustment to relatively novel situations by organising new psycho-physical co-ordination.
4. *Stern* defines intelligence as the general mental adaptability to new problems and conditions of life.
5. *William James* calls it the ability to adjust oneself successfully to a relatively novel situation.
6. *William McDougall* states "an intelligent action as one which seems to show that the creature has profited by prior experience of similar situations, that it somehow brings to bear its previous experience in the guidance of its present

action; intelligence is the capacity to improve upon native tendency in the light of past experience."

7. *Thorndike* defines it as, "We may define intelligence in general as the power of good responses from the point of view of truth or fact."
8. *Terman* writes: "An individual is intelligent in proportion as he is able to carry on abstract thinking."
9. *Num* regards it as the "flexibility of the mind to meet new situations."
10. *Boynton* states, "Intelligence is an inherited capacity of the individual which is manifested through his ability to adapt to and reconstruct the factors of his environment in accordance with the most fundamental needs of himself and his group."
11. *Johnson* thinks that intelligence stands for an "ability to solve the general run of human problems to adjust to new situations and in short the ability to think."
12. *Spearman* thinks intelligence in terms of two abilities, e.g., general ability or '*g*' and specific ability or '*s*'. Both kinds of abilities work in every performance. His '*g*' is the common factor which will colour every response, and his '*s*' is independent in every process. A scientist has two kinds of abilities, general as well as one specific for science. A musician has two kinds of abilities, general as well as specific, for music in this case. In the measurement of the intelligence of a person, both of these abilities should be taken into consideration.
13. *Vat Wagenen* treats intelligence as "capacity to learn and to adjust to relatively new and changing conditions."
14. *Freeman* writes, "Intelligence is represented in behaviour by the capacity of the individual to adjust himself to new situations to solve new problems to learn."
15. *Thurstone* stresses the "factorial analysis" theory which recognises intelligence as consisting of several abilities, seven of which have been identified:

    (i) number facility, (ii) word fluency, (iii) visualising, (iv) memory, (v) perceptual speech, (vi) induction, and (vii) verbal reasoning.

16. *Terman's* definition of Intelligence is on the following pattern—
    (i) Ability to carry on abstract thinking. This means, it cannot be manifested at the level of perception whereas in fact intelligence is involved in perceptual tasks.
    (ii) Capacity for abstract thinking, like all other abilities, involves factors specific to itself as well as intelligence.

This definition does not state that the abstract thinking is to be directed or relevant to a question or to some end.

Definitions: Classification of Intelligence

Broadly speaking there are three types of definitions regarding the meaning and development of intelligence.

(i) One group of definitions emphasises that intelligence is the ability to adjust, or adapt oneself to one's total environment or to limited aspects thereof—Burt, William James, McDougall, Goddard.

It is the capacity to organise one's behaviour pattern so as to act more effectively and more appropriately in novel situations. Thus, the more intelligent person could be one who can more easily and more extensively vary his behaviour as changing conditions demand.

(ii) The second type of definition states that intelligence is the ability to learn. Colvin is the propounder of this definition.

(iii) The third type of definition states that it is the ability to carry on abstract thinking—Binet, Terman and Freeman.

However, it would be very difficult to separate all these definitions into three clear-cut categories.

A definition of intelligence as the capacity to behave appropriately and effectively in new situations and a definition that intelligence is the ability to learn are in fact two aspects of the same process. Similarly, ability to carry on abstract thinking contributes to a person's ability to adjust or adapt to changing or new situations.

Wechsler's definition seems to combine and extend the three types of definitions. He states: "Intelligence is the aggregate global capacity of the individual to act purposefully, to think rationally and to deal effectively with his environment".

G.D. Stoddard offers the following definition: "Intelligence is the ability to undertake activities that are characterised by: 1. Difficulty, 2. Complexity, 3. Abstractness, 4. Economy, 5. Adaptiveness to a goal, 6. Social value, and 7. The emergence of originals and to maintain such activities under conditions that demand a concentration of energy and a resistance to emotional force."

OPERATIONAL DEFINITION AND MEANING OF INTELLIGENCE

Since theoretical discussions do not lead us to some precise nature of intelligence, Vernon states: "Intelligence is what intelligence tests measure".

Some argue, "We can measure electricity without being able to define its precise nature. But we can put electricity to use and measure it. So we can use and measure intelligence".

Now going into the discussion of these various definitions of intelligence, it may be said that intelligence is an ability to "see the right thing at the right moment in the right way." It is a general capacity to understand and meet with the situations that life may present, successfully. To quote Principal R.R. Kumria: "Call it practical wisdom; call it common sense; call it genius; it is just the same in different names and grades".

INTELLIGENCE AND SCHOLARS OF ANCIENT INDIA

Kautilya defines it as the ability to work.

According to Visnusarma, it is the power which enables human beings to control the world.

The *Brahmasutra* tells us that intelligence is the gift of God and it is fixed at birth.

The *Agnipurana* prescribes diet for infants to help the growth of their intelligence.

Types of Intelligence Accordance to Ancient View

Agadha buddhi or intelligence that cannot be measured or superior intelligence.

Mohabuddhi or great intelligence, *malin buddhi* or dull intelligence.

Sthira buddhi or calm intelligence.

Alpa buddhi or little intelligence.

In ancient India, intelligence was measured through conversation, physical features, gestures, gait, speech, changes in the eye and facial expression.

KINDS OF INTELLIGENCE AND A FEW GENERALISATIONS

Kinds of Intelligence

Thurstone has suggested three broad categories of intelligence:

1. *Abstract Intelligence*: He defined this as the "ability to understand and manage ideas and symbols, such as, words, number, chemical or physical formulas, legal decisions, scientific principles and the like. ..." In the case of students this is very close to what is called scholastic aptitude.
2. *Mechanical Intelligence*: This includes, "The ability to clean, to understand and manage things and mechanisms, such as, a knife, a gun, a moving machine, an automobile, a boat, a lathe..."
3. *Social Intelligence*: "This is the ability to understand and manage men and women, boys and girls to act wisely in human relations".

A Few Generalisations about Intelligence

Usually scholars, executives in business and Government, and scientists possess high abstract intelligence.

Mechanics, builders, expert carpenters and plumbers possess high mechanical intelligence.

High social intelligence is found in politicians, sales people and leaders in society.

A successful civil engineer presumably possesses high abstract as well as high mechanical intelligence; the successful criminal lawyer possesses abstract as well as social intelligence.

Distribution of Intelligence

The majority of the school children, say about 60%, are found in the I.Q. interval 90—110 and are referred to as 'Normal' or 'Average'.

Intelligence and Sex Differences: Generally speaking, the research studies show that the average scores of the sexes are strikingly similar.

Intelligence and Race Differences: Every racial and cultural group contains some gifted children. Franz Boas states, "If we were to select the most intelligent, imaginative, energetic and emotionally stable type of mankind, all races would be represented".

DEVELOPMENT OF INTELLIGENCE AND MENTAL TESTING

Intelligence cannot be increased or decreased. The amount of intelligence that a person possesses is inherited and fixed. The amount though fixed does not reveal itself at the start of life. With the growth of the child, the amount inherited by a child also grows. The general belief is that the growth of intelligence stops and it reaches its limit at the age of sixteen or seventeen. It is true that a man of forty knows more than a boy of sixteen. But this does not mean that the amount of intelligence possessed by him has increased. This may be due to his experience. As regards his intelligence, his position remains the same.

The growth of intelligence of certain children may be checked on account of certain unfavourable circumstances and when these are removed, intelligence begins to grow and functions normally.

An intelligent person has the ability to adjust himself to the changing circumstances with ease, efficiency and speed. He has the capacity to assimilate ideas very quickly and clearly. He can cope with new situations very successfully. All the inventions of the world can be attributed to persons of intelligence.

The unintelligent or the dullard individuals fail to think of new situations. They are always guided by others. They lack originality.

Are all persons equally intelligent? Are all the students fit for school instruction? Are all students capable of pursuing the same course? Are all students fit for all occupations? Is it proper to educate all students in the same way?

These and various such questions have been engaging the attention of the psychologists for the past hundred years or so. Many attempts have been made to measure intelligence possessed by individuals so that necessary arrangements may be made to give them training according to their intelligence. Thanks to the ceaseless efforts of various psychologists whose standardised tests are available which can be used to measure intelligence.

Psychological Testing

Anne Anastasi observes: "Psychological testing is a relatively young branch of one of the youngest of the sciences".

One of the first problems, which stimulated the development of psychological tests, was the identification of the feeble-minded. French physician *Esqurioi* was the first person to write a two-volume work in 1938 in which over one hundred pages were devoted to feeble-mindedness.

Another French physician who made a valuable contribution was *Seguin* who in 1837 established the first school devoted to the education of mentally defective children. In 1848 he migrated to America where his ideas gained recognition.

The general aim of the early experimental psychologists of the nineteenth century was the formulation of generalised description of human behaviour and not the measurement of individual differences. Many of the early experimental psychologists received their training in a laboratory founded by *Wundt* at Leipzig in 1879.

Sir Francis Galton, an English biologist, was primarily responsible for launching the testing movement on its course. In 1882, an anthropometric laboratory was established by him in South Kensington Museum, London. In this laboratory individuals could be measured in certain physical traits by the payment of a small fee. Galton himself devised most of the simple tests. Galton also paved the way for the application of rating scale and questionnaire methods etc. One of his disciples, Karl Pearson carried forward his work.

James McKeen Cattell of America occupies a prominent position in the development of psychological testing. He used the term "mental test" in an article in 1890. The article related a series of tests which were being administered annually to college students in the efforts to determine their intellectual level. Cattell like Galton felt that a measure of intellectual functions could be obtained through tests of sensory discrimination and reaction time.

Among others the names of *Jastrow*, *Krae Pelin* and *Ferrai* may also be mentioned.

The early experiments of Wundt were all concerned with sensory discrimination and motor ability. His worthy pupil Cattell did much useful work in America. However, the credit of scientific mental testing goes to Binet and Simon. The names of Terman and Cyril Burt may also be mentioned who did very useful work in mental testing.

In India, Dr. V.V. Kamat, Dr. C.H. Rice, Pt. L.S. Jha, Prof. S. Jalota and Principal R.R. Kumria have contributed a lot to psychological testing.

Landmarks in the Development of Testing

1826	Robert Owen's rating scale
1842	Seguin's form boards
1905	Binet-Simon scale
1908	Goddard translation of Binet's scale
1909	Court is practice test in arithmetic
1910	Thorndike handwriting scale
1911	Healy and Fernald performance test
1912	Hillegas composition scale
1913	Buckingham spelling scale
1915	Yerkes point scale
1916	Stanford revision of the Binet-Simon scale
1917	Army Group tests, Stenquist assembly tests
1919	Sea-shore tests of musical ability
1921	Rorschach test
1927	Strong vocational interest inventory
1933	Hildreth readiness tests
1935	Murray apperception test
1938	Thurstone primary abilities test

MEASUREMENT OF INTELLIGENCE

Intelligence is measured through a complicated process. It involves a comparison and establishment of a relationship between C.A. (Chronological Age) and M.A. (Mengal Age). This relationship is expressed by the term I.Q. (Intelligence Quotient). When the mental age is divided by the chronological age and the quotient is multiplied by 100, the result is I.Q.

$$\text{I.Q.} = \frac{\text{M.A.}}{\text{C.A.}} \times 100$$

BASIC CONCEPTS INVOLVED IN INTELLIGENCE AND INTELLIGENCE TESTING

1. *Chronological Age*: This refers to the age in years, months, hours. This is counted from the time and date of the birth of an individual. It is symbolically expressed as C.A.

2. *Mental Age* (*M.A.*): Binet was the first psychologist to introduce the concept of mental age. He gave a better footing and credibility to the intelligence test results. Alfred Binet was a French psychologist and an Education Officer. He is known as the father of Modern Psychological Testing. He was assisted by Simon and as such his intelligence test is known as Binet-Simon Test of Intelligence. The then French Government was faced with the problem of separating mentally retarded children from the normal ones. The job was assigned to Binet. It took about 15 years to complete the job. The year 1905 is a great landmark in the history of intelligence testing.

Menal age refers to '*Mental Maturity*' of a person. Corresponding to his level of performance in an intelligence test—irrespective of his C.A. If a person of C.A. 7 years old is able to score satisfactorily on a test meant for a child of C.A. 10, then the mental age (henceforth referred as M.A.) of the former is 10. Mental age can also be defined as an expression of the extent of development achieved by the individual stated in terms of the performance that can be expected at any given age".

And when the score of a given intelligence tests are put into M.A. scores—we have with us what is known as Age Scale. Maximum mental age is 19 or 20.

3. *Basal Age*: Basal age is that age of the child with reference to his chronological age where he can solve all questions in a given test. Mental age cannot be calculated directly. It is basal age which helps in the calculation of mental age.

This concept of basal age may be explained with the help of an example. There is a child with C.A. 6. He solves all questions in a test meant for child of C.A. 7. He also does the same for a child of C.A. 8 and then his efficiency declines, i.e., he solves only 2 questions out of 6 questions in a test meant for a child of C.A. 9. The basal age of a child with C.A. 6 is 8 years. His mental age will be

$$\text{Mental age} = \text{Basal age} + \text{partial credit}$$
$$= 8 \text{ years} + 4 \text{ months}$$

The child has an M.A. of $8\frac{1}{3}$ years

CLASSIFICATION OF INDIVIDUAL ON THE BASIS OF I.Q.

Terman's Classification

A. *On the basis of I.Q., Terman gives the following classification on American testees:*

Near genius or genius	Above 140
Very superior intelligence	120—140
Superior intelligence	110—120
Normal or average intelligence	90—110
Dullness	80—90
Borderline cases	70—80

Definite feeble-mindedness which has been further classified as under:

Morons	50—70
Imbeciles	25—50
Idiots	below 25

B. *Classification of Indian Children*

The Bombay-Karnataka Revision Tests: Dr. V.V. Kamat revised Binet's scale to suit Indian conditions and administered intelligence tests to 1,074 children and adolescents of all ages from 2 to 20 of both sexes.

The locality selected for the experiment was the town of Dharwar in the Bombay Presidency. The children selected were fairly representative of the general population of Indian children.

Dr. V.V. Kamat classifies Indian children as under:

Class	*Range of I.Q.s*
Near genius or genius	140 and above
Extraordinary	130—139.9
Very superior	120—129.9
Superior	110—119.9
Average or normal	99—109.9
Backward	80—98.9
Very backward	70—79.9
Borderline	60—69.9
Morons	40—59.9
Imbeciles	20—39.9
Idiots	Below 20

IMPORTANT USES OF INTELLIGENCE TESTS IN EVALUATION

Intelligence tests are very useful for the following purposes:

1. *Knowing Individual Differences among Learners*: Dr. V.V. Kamat has classified Indian children as above:
2. *Grouping in the Class*: Sometimes grouping in the class is done on the basis of intelligence test results.
3. *Classroom Teaching*: Intelligence tests enable the teacher to know the general mental level of the students and accordingly he adopts his teaching techniques.
4. *Identification of Slow Learners and the Gifted*: Intelligence tests help to identify learners in their capacity to learn. Accordingly enrichment programmes are provided to the gifted and compensatory/remedial education to the slow learners.
5. *Selection to Courses*: Different subjects require different degrees of intelligence. Some call for a higher order of intelligence and the others of a lower order.

   A nation-wide study in the U.S.A. gave the following Median I.Q. of the high school students in different courses:

Course	*Median I.Q.*
Technical	114.00
Scientific	108.00
Academic	106.00
Commerce	104.00
Trade	92.00

Burt found the following correlation between:

Intelligence and arithmetic (Problems)	0.65
Intelligence and the compositor	0.63
Intelligence and reading	0.56
Intelligence and spelling	0.52
Intelligence and writing	0.21
Intelligence and hard work	0.18
Intelligence and drawing	0.15

This implies that children of high I.Q. are superior in abstract thinking than those of low I.Q.

6. *Selection in Occupations*: Burt draws up the following provisional scheme for occupational classification according to the degree of intelligence occupations require:

S.No.	*Occupation*	*I.Q. Require*
1.	Higher professional and administrative work—Lawyer, physician, architect, teacher (University and Secondary level)	150
2.	Lower professional technical and executive work	130 to 150
3.	Clerical and highly skilled work—shorthand, typist, bank clerk, salesman, electrician, nurse	115 to 130
4.	Skilled work—tailor, dressmaker, carpenter, cashier, printer	100 to 115
5.	Semi-skilled repetitive work—barber, welder, miner, painter, banker	85 to 100
6.	Unskilled repetitive work—manual labour	70 to 85
7.	Casual labour—simplest routine work	50 to 75

7. *Promotion*: Intelligence tests are used for the promotion of students to the next class.

7. *Selection of Students to a School*: In good schools, there is always rush for admission. All the applicants though eligible for admission cannot be admitted. It then becomes necessary to adopt some additional methods of selection. Intelligence tests help to meet out this difficulty to a considerable extent. By administering these tests, authorities pick out the innately brighter boys.
8. *The Discovery of Unusual Cases*: The lack of intelligence may be the main cause of abnormal behaviour. The intelligence tests help to find out cases of abnormal behaviour.
9. *Intelligence and Success in College*: Gates and others think that an I.Q. of at least 120 is needed to do acceptable college work in a first class college with an average expenditure of time and energy.
10. *Help in Diagnosis of Backwardness*: Ordinary scholastic examinations fail to discover 'educable abilities'. The failure of a child in the examination is no indication that he lacks intelligence. This failure may be on account of defective methods of teaching or it may be due to some temperamental or physical obstacles which might have stood in the way of the child. There may not be any fault with the intelligence of the child only it has not been allowed to work itself out.
11. *Award of Scholarship*: Various public scholarships are awarded on the basis of the results secured through intelligence tests. The Government of India selects some students for the award of scholarships for studying in Public Schools on the basis of the intelligence and achievement tests.
12. *Evaluation of Methods and Materials of Instruction*: Intelligence Tests are helpful in evaluating the results of the experiments conducted by a school in the relative importance of the different methods of instruction i.e., achievement obtained with different text-books or with a certain text-book as contrasted with extensive reading material not confined to any one book.
13. *Assessment of Teacher's Work*: When the achievement of the pupils in a subject does not correspond to the scores of intelligence tests, it gives indication to the fact that the

subject has not been properly taught by the teacher and properly understood by the students.

Limitations of Intelligence Tests

It would be a great mistake to think that these tests are all in all in measuring the various aspects of the learner's personality. Intelligence is one of the factors. Too much reliance cannot be made on this evaluation tool. It is to be used in conjunction with other tools. Following are the important limitations of intelligence tests:

1. Intelligence tests seek to measure intelligence which in itself is not a clear concept. Psychologists differ radically on the meaning and nature of intelligence.
2. Intelligence tests fail to measure the depth, strength, weakness and quality of an individual relating to his emotional stability.
3. Intelligence tests fail to evaluate the ethical, moral and spiritual qualities of an individual.
4. Intelligence test do not take into account the environmental factors. The test may include items/material with which the children of socio-economic groups have more experience than those of weaker sections.
5. Use of intelligence tests need a good deal of care and caution on the part of the test administrator/user.

14

Personality

In simple language by personality, we mean the totality of everything about an individual—his emotional, ethical, mental, physical, social and spiritual make-up. It includes an individual's appearance, emotionality, sociability, intelligence, character and moral traits.

The term 'personality' is derived from a Latin word '*Persona*' which means the mask worn by a Roman actor. In this sense personality means the individual as seen by others. Personality thus implies the cover-up of the real person. One actor plays several roles. In other words, personality is taken to refer to the outward aspect of the individual which actually does not mean anything except in theatre.

COMPLEX NATURE OF PERSONALITY AND DEFINITIONS OF PERSONALITY

As observed by Murphy (1947), "We do not believe that anyone today can seriously understand to say that he knows what personality is." Present situation also seems to be very unclear, although no topic in the field of psychology is more fascinating than personality. Volumes have been written on the topic, yet we are unable to say clearly what personality is.

Earlier in 1937, G.W. Allport, who had done a good deal of research on personality, mentioned fifty-three definitions of personality in his book "*Personality: A Psychological Interpretation*". Since then how many definitions have been added is any body's guess!

Following are some of the definitions of personality:

1. According to *R.B. Cattell*, "Personality is that which permits a prediction of what a person will do in a given situation."

2. In the words of *L.J. Cronbach*, "Character is not really a cumulation of separate habits and ideas, character is embedded in the total structure of personality."
3. *J.F. Dashiell*, states: "Personality is the sum total of behaviour trends manifested in social adjustments."
4. In the opinion of *J.P. Guilford*: 'An individual's personality is his unique pattern of traits".
5. *Healy William* describes personality as "an integrated system of habitual adjustment to environment particularly to social environment.
6. *Kurt Lewin*, considers personality as "a dynamic totality of systems."
7. *Mortem Prince* thinks personality as "the sum total of biological innate dispositions, impulses, tendencies, aptitudes and instincts of the individual and the dispositions and tendencies acquired by experience."
8. In the words of *R.M. Ogsten*, "Personality is the expression of man's inner life, character is the expression of what he does or achieves."
9. According to *G.W. Allport*, "Personality is the dynamic organisation within the individual of those psycho-physical systems that determine his unique adjustment to the environment."
10. *Woodworth* gives the following definition, "Personality is the '*total*' quality of an individual's behaviour as it is revealed in his characteristics habits of thought and expression, his attitudes and interests, his manner of acting and his personal philosophy of life.
11. *Eysenck's* definition of personality is as follows, "Personality is the more or less stable and enduring organisation of a person's character, temperament, intellect and physique, which determine his unique adjustment to environment.
12. *S.R. Maddi*, an American psychologist in his work, '*Personality Theories—A Comparative Analysis*' (1976), one of the latest analysis has defined personality as, "Personality is the stable set of characteristics and tendencies that determine those commonalities and differences in the psychological behaviour (thoughts, feelings and action) of

people that have continuity in time and that may or may not be easily understood in terms of the social and biological pressure of the immediate situation alone."

Evaluation of Definitions

A perusal of the above definitions would indicate that the definition given by Eysenck (H.J.) seems to be quite functional and operational. It has the following merits.

First. It takes into consideration a balanced view of the conative behaviour or will, affective behaviour based on emotions and cognitive behaviour—intellect or intelligence. Thus this definition attempts to give a complete picture of human behaviour by involving all of its three aspects—Conative, Cognition and affective.

Second. It accords appropriate consideration to the physiological aspect of the personality of an individual.

Third. It emphasises the need to integrate the behaviourist characteristics.

Fourth. It makes personality somewhat assessable and measurable.

However, this definition has one important weakness. It may not be stable in the sense that some circumstances may bring about radical changes in the character and other aspects of an individual. The world is moving so fast that in the span of life of an individual, he may be required to change his behaviour pattern altogether to adjust himself to the changed environment.

Some scholars consider Allport's definition to be comprehensive and clear. It lays stress on these characteristics of personality: (i) Dynamic nature, (ii) Heredity and environment, (iii) Wholeness.

CHARACTERISTICS AND NATURE OF PERSONALITY

From the definitions given above, following characteristics of personality emerge very clearly:

1. Personality is what one is.
2. Personality of each individual is unique.
3. Personality is dynamic and not static.
4. Personality functions as a unified whole.

5. Personality is the product of both heredity and environment.
6. Personality is through and through social.
7. Personality is continually adjusting itself to environment.
8. In rare cases personality influences the environment.
9. Personality is always striving for certain ends.
10. Personality is self-consciousness. We do not attribute personality to animals.
11. Personality is influenced by the school environment.
12. It is only through the study of personality of individual students, that the relative differences among them can be known and their personality developed to the optimum level.

BEHAVIOURAL PATTERNS OF PERSONALITY

The totality of a man's personality may be described as under:

1. The attitude of an individual with which he does some work.
2. The skill of an individual with which he does a job.
3. The way he acts.
4. The way he behaves.
5. The way he dresses.
6. The way he drinks and eats.
7. The way he sits and stands.
8. The way he speaks.
9. The way he walks and so on.

MARKS OF BALANCED DEVELOPMENT OF PERSONALITY

1. Good physical appearance.
2. Emotional stability.
3. High intellectual ability.
4. High degree of social adjustment.
5. High moral character.
6. Cool temperament.
7. Good directedness.
8. High adjustability.
9. Tremendous common sense, drive and pragmatic thinking.

Classification or Types of Personality

Following are the important types of personality:

Type	*Author*
1. Active and Inactive	Heymans
2. Active and Reflective	Jordan
3. Extrovert and Introvert	C.G. Ung
4. Masculine and Feminine	Apfelback
5. Romantic and Classical	Ostwald
6. Stable and Unstable	Trotler
7. Subjective and Objective	Binet
8. Tender minded and Tough minded	William James

Spranger's Six Types of Personality

1. *Aesthetic*: Lovers of beauty.
2. *Economic*: Inclined to hoard money.
3. *Political*: Interested in political affairs.
4. *Religious*: Believer in mysticism and engaged in religious activities.
5. *Social*: Interested in social affairs.
6. *Theoretical*: Theoretical in nature.

DEVELOPMENT OF PERSONALITY: BIOLOGICAL AND SOCIO-CULTURAL DETERMINANTS

See on next page.

Physique: In physique are included such factors as the appearance, strength, body-build, bodily proportions, colouring and physical beauty of the individual. These factors have direct as well as indirect influence on the development of personality. Deformity handicaps the child both physically and psychologically. Fewer physically handicapped develop into normal personalities. Health and vigour are significant in early years since contacts and competitions among children are often on the physical level. Even in adult years, the man with a tough constitution is at an advantage in maintaining an aggressive attitude towards life and preserving his emotional balance.

Development of Personality: Biological and Socio-cultural Determinants

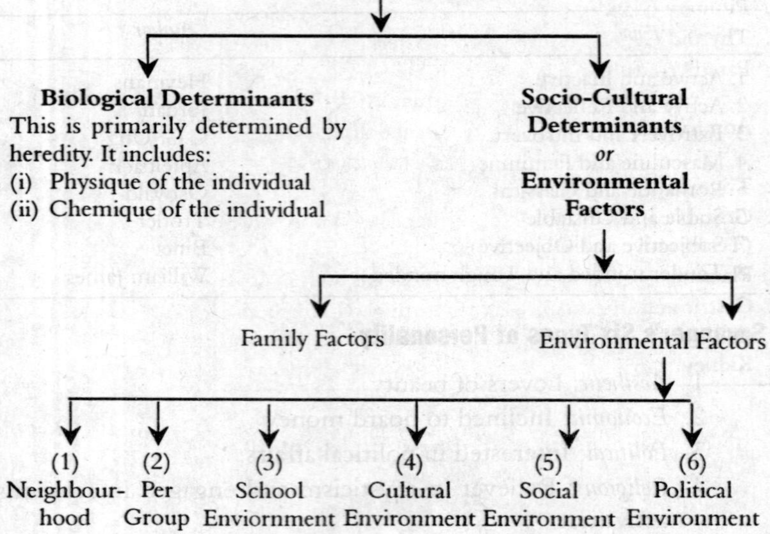

Chemique: By chemique is meant the possible effects of the ductless glands on the personality development. Glands are small organs which change chemical substances from one form to another in the body.

Endocrine (Ductless Glands)

Meaning: The endocrine glands bring about chemical coordination by complex organic compounds called 'hormones'. Hormones are chemical regulators or chemical messengers of body. These are secreted in response to changes in the environment inside or outside the body. Hormones are secreted by specialised glands. These lack definite ducts for the transportation of their secretion but pour them directly into the blood. Therefore, these glands are called ductless glands or endocrine glands (glands of internal secretion).

Endocrine Glands in Man

Name of Gland	*Location*
1. Pituitary Gland	In head (on underside of fore brain)
2. Thyroid Gland	In neck-(across the front of wind pipe)
3. Parathyroids (4)	One at each of the outer corners of thyroid
4. Adrenals (2)	In abdominal—(across the upper end of each kidney)
5. Thymus	
6. Gonads or Sex Glands (Testes and ovaries)	In or below the pelvic cavity
7. Placenta	Pregnant uterus
8. Gastric and Intestinal mucosa	In the abdominal cavity (in the wall of stomach and intestine)
9. Kidney	In the abdominal cavity kidney cell

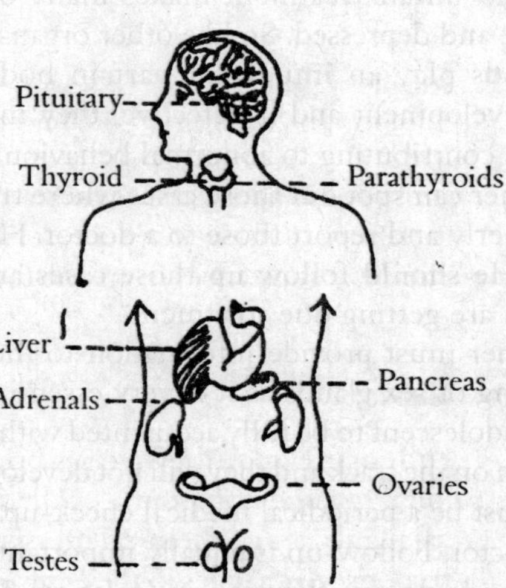

Fig. 14.1: Location of Ductless Glands

Educational Implications of Endocrine and Ductless Glands

These glands have a direct bearing on the personality of an individual. Actually, there are the hormones secreted by these glands which play an important role. These hormones are circulated throughout the body and influence all those tissues on which the functioning of body system, emotional actions and even thoughts depend. As Murphy, Gardner (1968) has observed, "these harmones, ultimately may be regarded as bathing the nervous system, including the brain, and all the organs of the body in their own appropriate chemical juices."

If the thyroid gland is overactive, it results in nervousness, dizziness and difficulty in sleeping.

Sex glands or gonads are responsible for sex drive or urge. The effects of the sex glands on emotions, particularly personality and behaviour become specially significant when adolescence is reached.

The individuals with profound imbalance of ductless glands are rarely happy or well-adjusted. They suffer from apathy, anxiety, restlessness, fatigue, irritability, etc. It is not easy for certain bearded ladies and gents to remain good-natured and mentally serene when they are continuously exposed to ridicule, jest, and social isolation. This harsh and unfair treatment makes many of them morose, hypersensitive and depressed. So like other organs of the body, the ductless glands play an important part in bodily, mental and emotional, development and if defective, they may constitute an added burden contributing to abnormal behaviour.

The teacher can spot out those cases where the glands are not working properly and report those to a doctor. His duty does not finish here. He should follow up those cases and see to it that such children are getting due treatment.

The teacher must provide information to the adolescents on the functioning of sex glands as it is very essential for the mental health of the adolescent to be fully acquainted with this aspect. This will keep them on the track and they will not develop wrong notions.

There must be a periodical medical check-up in the school by a qualified doctor. Follow-up is equally important.

These glands do not function in isolation. If they are active normally, they give rise to a balanced personality. In case they are under-active or overactive, they may lead to personality problems and even abnormalities.

Family Factors

These are: (i) Discipline: Protection and rejection etc. (ii) Number of children, (iii) Value placed on the sex of the child, (iv)

Step-parents, (v) Nuclear or joint family, (vi) Accommodation in the house, (vii) Parents' ambitions and interests, (viii) Economic, political, religious and social status of the family.

School Environment: This includes:

(i) Curriculum;
(ii) Technology of teaching;
(iii) Co-curricular activities;
(iv) Discipline—constructive, creative and social;
(v) Teachers' personality and their behaviour towards students;
(vi) General tone of the school; and
(vii) Physical environment.

BARRIERS IN THE DEVELOPMENT OF INTEGRATED PERSONALITY

See on next page.

INTEGRATION OF PERSONALITY AND THE ROLE OF THE SCHOOL

Meaning of Integration of Personality

Just as a building is more than bricks, cement and wood; similarly, personality is more than basic elements or parts. Personality is formed because of the special relationship among its parts. Personality has an integrated structure (Fig. 14.2) . Any change in one part of the structure influences other parts.

Development of the following aspects of the personality must be fully integrated. Unbalanced development of any one of the aspects has an adverse impact on the total development of personality.

(i) Physical structure of the individual,
(ii) Emotional reactions,
(iii) Aspirations,
(iv) Aptitudes,
(v) Attitudes,
(vi) Interests,
(vii) Motivation,
(viii) Intellectual level—thinking, contemplation, reasoning, etc.

Barriers in the Development of Integrated Personality

- **Family Circumstances**
  - *Economic*
    - (i) Problem of unemployment or semi-employment
    - (ii) Low economic status
  - *Psychologieal*
    - (i) Over possessive parents
    - (ii) Unrealistic expectations from childrens
    - (iii) Faulty home discipline
    - (iv) Use of abusive language
    - (v) Lack of role model parents
    - (vi) Unequal parental treatment to siblings
    - (vii) Fear of insecurity
  - *Social*
    - (i) Loss of social status of the family
    - (ii) Broken homes
    - (iii) Fear of insecurity
    - (iv) Some anti-social stigma to the family
- **Personal**
  - Some physical defects
- **School**
  1. Unattractive school environment
  2. Unsuitable curriculum or wrong choice of subjects
  3. Lack of curricular activities
  4. Lack of discipline
- **Teachers**
  1. Unsympathetic teachers
  2. Emotinally unstable teachers
- **Peers**
  1. Undesirable interests and activities of peers
  2. Non-acceptance in the group

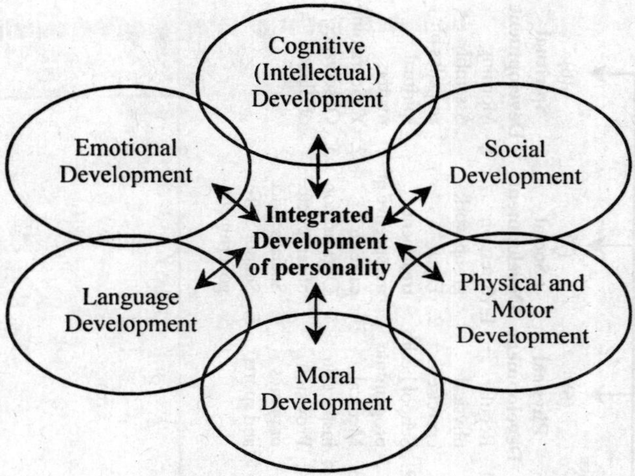

Fig. 14.2: Integrated Personality

Role of the School in the Development of Integrated Personality

An individual of a well-integrated personality is aesthetically refined, culturally rich, emotionally stable, intellectually sound, physically strong, politically wide-awake, religiously pious, socially efficient, spiritually enlightened and vocationally self-sufficient.

Role of the Teachers in Personality Development of the Students

1. Teacher as a 'Spiritual Preceptor' as in the Vedic Period.
2. Teacher as a 'Communicator and Provider of Knowledge'.
3. Teacher as a 'Living Facilitator'.
4. Teacher as a 'Gardener' or 'Directress' of Learning in the Naturalist Movement in Education.
5. Teacher as a 'Manager' of learning activity in the Pragmatic Philosophy of Education.
6. Teacher as an 'Ideal Person' in the Philosophy of Idealism.
7. Teacher as a 'Soldier' and 'Weapon' in Nazism and Communism.
8. Teacher as an 'Agent of Social Change' in the Democratic Philosophy.
9. Teacher as a 'Mediator' between the learner and the subject-matter.

Chart: School Programmes for the Development of an Integrated Personality of the Learner

(1) Aesthetic Development	(2) Cognitive Development	(3) Emotional Development	(4) Ethical Development	(5) Language Development	(6) Physical Development	(7) Social Development	(8) Spiritual Development
1. Provision of attractive and beautiful physical development. 2. All-round Individual	1. Psychological methods of teaching–learning 2. Provision of varied instructional material 3. Satisfaction of the individual needs	1. Balanced personality of the teacher 2. Environment of love and affection 3. Appropriate disciplinary approach	1. Personal example of the teacher 2. Social Service activities	1. Correct modes of expression by the teacher. 2. Proper check on pronunciation of the students 3. Provision of rich language material	1. Regular physical exercise 2. School health programme 3. Medical inspection 4. Provision of games and sports	1. Stress on group work 2. Equal treatment irrespective of caste etc. 3. Organisation of camps etc. 4. Social service 5. School Self-government	1. Morning Assembly and talks on spiritual matters 2. Yogic training 3. Observance of silance.

10. Teacher as a 'Transmitter' of cultural heritage.
11. Teacher as the 'Educational Media User.'
12. Teacher as the 'Spearhead' of change in the society.
13. Teacher as the 'Harbinger' of social change.

Character and Personality of the Teacher: Character and personality of the pupils cannot be developed if the teacher who is the model to be followed lacks character and personality. 'Example is better than precept' is an old saying and is absolutely true in the teaching profession. No amount of sermons from the teacher can make much headway. A teacher teaches not only by 'what he says and does' but very largely by 'what he is'.

'Man Know Thyself' is the advice of Yajnavalkya in India and by Socrates of Greece. The teachers must undergo a spiritual inner training. They should try to find out their own shortcomings and remove them. Ryburn has observed: "Self-analysis on the part of a teacher is a necessary equipment". Montessory stresses that "every teacher worth his salt must destroy these sins: pride, anger, sloth, sensuality and envy. He should be partly a doctor, partly a scientist and completely religious. He must acquire a moral alertness, patience, love and humility". Writing about the role of the teachers, Lauri has observed: "If a teacher has not an ideal aim, he had better to take to shopkeeping at once, he will there doubtless find an ideal within his capacity."

Summing up: There is a limit to the role of the school in the integrated development of the personality of the learner. In the ultimate analysis, it must be stressed that the overall environment of the society has a great bearing on the development of the personality of the learners. In this regard, a great responsibility lies on the role of the leaders, especially political and religious.

15

Suggestive Guidelines for Teachers for the Optimum Development and Education of the Students

These guidelines are to refresh the teachers, inspire them, encourage them and to give proper perspectives for coping with the challenges they face each day both in and out of the classroom. These need to be kept in mind while doing any work.

- Each child has the potential to bloom.
- The best way to develop children is to develop oneself.
- The best way to teach is to learn.
- Realise the dignity of your calling.
- Never threaten the learners.
- Obstacles present choices.
- Use of knowledge is as important as the knowledge itself.
- Curiosity is the seed of knowledge, it must be awakened in the learners.
- Anger is the logical expression of frustration.
- Don't just teach.
- Learn to balance yourself.
- The best example is experience.
- Let early education be a sort of amusement; you will then be able to find out the natural bent of the learners.
- Approach each day with humour.
- Love the learner and the learner will love you.

- Be at peace with yourself before endeavouring to bring peace to others.
- To be a teacher is to wear many hats.
- Children are most interested in those who are interested in them.
- Constant criticism of learners breads despair.
- Hardwork leads to greatness.
- Focus on solutions, not problems.
- A vision without action is but a dream.
- Repetition combined with understanding creates permanent memories.
- Consistent discipline is appreciated and honoured.
- Self-analysis and follow up would pay dividends.
- Manage your time.
- Be gentle, kind and soft but not confused.
- Have a true passion for your subject.
- When teachers turn the key of motivation, they will get much more mileage from the class.
- No matter how often the teacher uses the same brushes and paints, each canvas (student) will be different.
- The difference between memorising and learning is understanding.
- Behaviour is controlled by us, we are not controlled by behaviour.
- Avoid ego as it is the greatest obstacle to reality.
- Make no judgments before tests.
- No single test is an absolute measure of accomplishment.
- In anger and in peace, choose your words.
- Touch children's heart and you will be remembered.
- Touch a child's mind and you will be venerated.
- Students glean much more from actions than from your words.

- Knowledge is never a substitute for experience.
- When authority does not allow children to question anything, the children will question authority.
- It is wonderful when children learn that they can ask questions without fear.
- Interacting with all students during a lesson is the best way to find out how they are doing.
- Seek the promise of the future in the lessons of the past.
- Maturity is achieved when experience becomes the basis for decision.
- Always be positive.
- Courtesy costs nothing; it is the stepladder to respect.
- Self control is a function of self-discipline.
- Be strong and you can bend. Be rigid and you will break.
- Kindness is the one gift that all can afford and all can repay.
- Personality is the clothing, character is the soul.
- The ability to take responsibility is a true sign of strength.
- Community is the basic lesson of the classroom.
- A child can learn strength only from someone who is strong.
- The map of progress has no straight roads.
- When the quest for knowledge ceases, the mind and spirit die.
- Excitement is the bait on teacher hook. If you are to catch the students interest, excite their appetite.
- The great art of teaching consists of knowing how to occupy every moment of teaching-learning.
- A mother gives birth to the child, a teacher gives birth to the mind.
- Order in the classroom depends on self-discipline.
- A teacher who demonstrates character builds character.
- All children begin as children, adult perspective should not be imposed.

- Learning without thought is labour lost; thought without learning is perilous.
- The teacher who loves to learn is an exciting teacher.
- When one stops learning one stops growing.
- For teachers; it is better to get questions than answers.
- Teach students how to ask questions in a manner that leads to the answers.
- Let children learn by stimulating their natural sense of wonder in the world.
- The way to teach the value of life is to 'live' life.
- The mediocre teacher tells. The good teacher explains. The superior teacher demonstrates. The great teacher inspires.
- Welcome new ideas.
- Teach independence in conjunction with obedience.

A TO Z OF TEACHING COMPETENCIES AND SKILLS WHICH MAKE TEACHING-LEARNING EFFECTIVE

- 'A' is for alertness.
- 'B' is for business like attitude—keeping students and himself busy in worthwhile tasks.
- 'C' is for cooperative teaching-learning and clarity of the subject matter.
- 'D' is for devotion to work and discovering students' potential.
- 'E' is for enthusiasm expecting children to learn, and evaluating them properly.
- 'F' is for feedback for the guidance of the learner and the teacher himself.
- 'G' is for goal setting and achieving.
- 'H' is for hard work and honest work, humility and humour.
- 'I' is for involvement of children.
- 'J' is for judicious attitude, just action and judicious use of praise and blame.
- 'K' is for knowledge of the students, subject matter and oneself.

- 'L' is for linking learning with previous learning experience, with daily experience and life activities.
- 'M' is for motivation.
- 'N' is for need-based learning and creating novel situations for learning.
- 'O' is for objectivity and providing out-of-classroom learning experiences.
- 'P' is for patience and praising children when needed.
- 'Q' is for quiz-organising for monitoring learning process and appropriate technique of questioning.
- 'R' is for relationships and review.
- 'S' is for stimulation.
- 'T' is for tolerance and the technology of teaching-learning.
- 'U' is for unbiased attitude and unexpected encounters and situations and facing them efficiently.
- 'V' is for a variety of learning experiences.
- 'W' is for warmth for the students.
- 'X' is for x-ray of the teaching-learning process.
- 'Y' is for yearning and eagerness for the improvement of teaching-learning.
- 'Z' is for zeal for the optimum development of the learners.